Dario Fo

Dario Fo

Framing, Festival, and the Folkloric Imagination

Antonio Scuderi

LEXINGTON BOOKS
Lanham • Boulder • New York • Toronto • Plymouth, UK

Published by Lexington Books
A wholly owned subsidiary of The Rowman & Littlefield Publishing Group, Inc.
4501 Forbes Boulevard, Suite 200, Lanham, Maryland 20706
http://www.lexingtonbooks.com

Estover Road, Plymouth PL6 7PY, United Kingdom

Copyright © 2011 by Lexington Books

Frontispiece: Sketch of the backdrop for *The Holy Jester Francis*, by Dario Fo

All rights reserved. No part of this book may be reproduced in any form or by any electronic or mechanical means, including information storage and retrieval systems, without written permission from the publisher, except by a reviewer who may quote passages in a review.

British Library Cataloguing in Publication Information Available

Library of Congress Cataloging-in-Publication Data
Scuderi, Antonio, 1956–
 Dario Fo : framing, festival, and the folkloric imagination / Antonio Scuderi.
  p. cm.
 Includes bibliographical references and index.
 ISBN 978-0-7391-5111-2 (cloth : alk. paper)
 1. Fo, Dario—Criticism and interpretation. 2. Fo, Dario—Technique. 3. Fo, Dario—Stage history. 4. Theater—Italy—History—20th century. I. Title.
 PQ4866.O2Z844 2011
 852'.914—dc22   2011017955

♾™ The paper used in this publication meets the minimum requirements of American National Standard for Information Sciences—Permanence of Paper for Printed Library Materials, ANSI/NISO Z39.48-1992.

Printed in the United States of America

This book is dedicated to my father Luciano Scuderi and to the memory of my mother Angela Scuderi.

Contents

Acknowledgments ix

1 Introduction, Scope, and Methodology 1

2 Metacommunication and the Interpretive Frame 9

3 Ennobling Folk Culture and Re-Presenting History 35

4 The European Carnival from Liminal to *Liminoid* 53

5 The Carnival Frame and Zoomorphic Symbolism 77

6 Dario Fo and *The Holy Jester Francis* 97

Works Cited 131
Index 143

Acknowledgments

The research and writing that went into this study was greatly facilitated by a sabbatical leave that was granted to me by Truman State University. Friends and colleagues generously helped with proofreading, suggestions, and feedback. These include Gloria Allaire, Joe Benevento, Adam Davis, Joe Farrell, and Helena Kaufman. Two former professors at the University of Wisconsin–Madison offered advice in their specialized fields: Thomas D. Cravens in linguistics and Christopher Kleinhenz in medieval studies and Dante. Special thanks to folklorist Richard Bauman, who was kind enough to read the manuscript, offer sage advice, and suggest the title.

The present study includes, in greatly expanded forms, three previously published articles (Scuderi 2003, 2004, and 2005). Permission to reprint from these was granted by *Theatre Journal* (The Johns Hopkins University Press), *Modern Language Review* (Modern Humanities Research Association), and *New Theatre Quarterly* (Cambridge University Press). Giulio Einaudi editore granted permission to quote extensively from Dario Fo's *Lu santo jullàre Françesco*. Dario Fo, Franca Rame, Jacopo Fo, and their competent staff were gracious in granting permission to quote from Dario's plays and from the interviews he gave me. They also provided me with original artwork by Dario, as well as permission to reproduce them. Thanks also to artist and photographer Brent Orton who enlarged and enhanced the electronic image of Fo's sketch for the frontispiece. All translations are by me, unless otherwise indicated.

Chapter One

Introduction, Scope, and Methodology

For Dario Fo the 1997 Nobel Prize for Literature was the crowning moment of a career that spans over half a century. Rarely in the history of theatre does a talent like Fo come along. His satirical farces, which have been translated into dozens of languages, continue to be among the most often performed plays throughout the world, and at any given moment there are productions in various countries on various continents. In addition to his popularity as a playwright, his skill and power as a performer are legendary. As an outlet for his extraordinary stage talents he developed his *giullarata* (pl. –e), named for the *giullare*, Italian for "jongleur," the itinerant performer of the Middle Ages. In this special brand of one-man show, without costumes or props, Fo holds audiences spellbound as he simultaneously narrates and acts, accompanied by his remarkable gestural language. This is true even when he performs abroad with an on-stage interpreter. While his satirical farces enjoy tremendous international popularity, in Italy his *giullarate* have inspired a new generation of solo performers.[1]

Fo's involvement with theatre goes beyond his accomplishments as a playwright and actor. Continuing the Italian tradition of an actor-dominated theater, in which actors applied themselves to all aspects of their trade, he directs, designs sets and costumes, and choreographs his own productions. These skills, as well as his extensive knowledge of historical theatrical devices, have been showcased in various productions of Rossini operas. Fo's productions of Rossini have been staged in Paris, Amsterdam, Helsinki, and other European cities. He is also a visual artist in his own right, and his paintings and drawings have garnered the attention of art critics.[2] His artwork is often incorporated in his performances and adorns his books and published plays. He has also written books and produced television documentaries on Italian artists and art history. At the time this study was being prepared, Fo was in his eighties. Though he can no longer sustain very lengthy performances (he seems to be limiting himself to one hour), his level of theatrical activity is still impressive, and he is dedicating more time to writing books.

Over the years, assisted by his wife and long-time collaborator, actress Franca Rame,[3] Fo developed a unique and idiomatic way of creating and presenting theatre. Some aspects of this are by now well known. He does not simply write a script that is ready to be rehearsed and performed. He begins with a skeletal outline or a fully scripted text, either of which is developed and greatly modified throughout the rehearsal process. When working with an ensemble of actors (rather than on his one-man show), rehearsals may seem rather chaotic. At any moment Fo will call a stop to the action in order to make changes to the ever evolving text. Frequently, updated scripts must be passed out to the actors. Modifications continue throughout the show's run, based on audience response, and often current events, if relevant, are worked in as well. This way of creating a play rejects the supremacy of the written text (which explains, in part, why some people in the literary world were outraged when he was awarded the Nobel). Instead, a Fo play develops through a dialectical process between text and performance.

Dario Fo introduces each performance with an extended prologue, which calls for the audience's attention but is not yet the performance proper. This begins to blur the line between performing and not performing, and allows him to move in and out of character. In this way, he intends to put the emphasis on the story he and his actors will convey, rather than on the characters they will be portraying. Another function of the prologue is to provide the audience with background to the story and underscore the messages Fo wishes to impart. These messages, which are the heart and soul of his performances, comprise an intricate network of interlocking themes and leitmotifs that refer to and interact with each other across his plays. They are an essential part of all the elements that come together organically to constitute Fo's *theatre*. His theatre is a microcosm, based on a world according to Fo, defined by a struggle between popular and official cultures. This microcosm exists in a carnivalesque liminality, where world order is suspended, and he blurs the line between fact and fiction.

Introduction, Scope, and Methodology

Rather than moving diachronically across Fo's long career, the present study is organized thematically, with no attempt being made to fit his works into any theoretical rubric. Instead the analytical strategy is to follow Fo's own lead. His own intellectual interests and some of the scholars who influenced him, directly or indirectly over the years, have suggested the analytic tools of investigation. The focus is on three interrelated aspects of Dario Fo's theatre. First, by way of repeating and interconnecting his major themes, he creates an intricate thematic or indexical *frame* (discussed below and in the following chapter). Then by employing various methods, including metanarrational and metatheatrical techniques, he refers to this frame to underscore the social and political messages he means to convey. Second, he is known to invent information which he presents under the guise of facts. He does this mostly through his re-presentation of history, which is an important part of his theatre. Third, whether contextualized in the past or in the present, his presentation of social and political issues is animated by European carnival culture. Based on his interpretation of prehistory and anthropology, the carnival frame informs his entire corpus from the 1960s on.

Fo (b. 1926) has often pointed to the influence of the *fabulatori*, storytellers of his childhood, in the lake region of northern Italy. In his autobiography he explains how, at a certain point, he began to make the connection between the verbal art of these popular performers and conventional notions of theater:

> Those *fabulatori* did not conceive of narration as theatre, and neither did I at that time connect the two genres. Above all, I was not yet able to reconcile the great difference between narrating and performing. I was absolutely convinced that making theatre exclusively implied acting along with other actors, set design, lighting and sound effects, in short, organized magic. Only later, after I had acquired a considerable degree of experience on stage, I understood that storytelling had been the mechanism that motivated me to express myself in a popular-epic form. (2002:60)

In this passage Fo uses *epic* with reference to the theory of theatrical performance, as developed by Erwin Piscator and especially Bertolt Brecht. When used in this context in the present study, it will always be indicated as "epic theatre." The term *epic* will also be used in the context of epic tales, such as in the Homeric tradition or the tradition of the Serbo-Croatian ballad singers, studied by Milman Parry and Albert Lord.

As a champion of popular culture, Fo borrowed and developed many techniques from traditional and oral modes of performance. Chapter 2 is an analysis of narrative and theatrical elements derived from these traditions. At the basis of the analysis is the concept of framing, which began in behavioral psychology and sociology, and was taken up and adapted by folklore performance studies. One of the most important books in the field is Richard Bauman's *Verbal Art as Performance*. Following in the footsteps of scholars such the linguistic anthropologist Dell Hymes, Bauman takes the concept of performance beyond the confines of formal theatre and adapts it to popular narrative. Viewed through the lens of *Verbal Art*, it becomes clear that Fo has intuited many of the mechanisms that are at work in popular modes. Thus concepts such as performance frame and interpretive frame are effective tools of analysis for Fo's theatre.

Also in the tradition of Parry and Lord, the work of John Miles Foley on oral narrative provides an approach for understanding the thematic or *indexical* frame. Foley has argued convincingly that in certain oral traditions an indexical frame allows a performer to refer to narrative elements that reach beyond the context of the performance at hand. Without working within a living oral tradition, Fo has managed to reconstruct a similar mechanism. This second chapter looks closely at his use of framing in a mature work, *The Two-Headed Anomaly*. This satirical farce, produced in 2003, is aimed at Prime Minister Silvio Berlusconi, who, as a powerful politician and media mogul, managed to keep the play from being broadcast on major European television channels. Berlusconi's action stands as testament to the efficacy of Fo's unique brand of farcical satire. Chapter 2 ends by picking up some of the major themes of the indexical frame that were referred to in *Anomaly*, and tracing how they were established and used in other plays.

Chapter 3 takes up the function of history, one of the most difficult aspects of Fo studies. In his theatre, history is combination of a legitimate analysis, reevaluation, and rethinking of history on the one hand, and a blatant manipulation of facts on the other. The result is an eccentric re-presentation of history. Undoubtedly, Fo was influenced by his reading of the social philosopher, Antonio Gramsci, who adapted principles of Marxism to the specific situation in Italy of his day. Gramsci's concepts, such as hegemony and the role of the intellectual, are at the basis of Fo's social and political worldview, and it could be argued that, in many ways, Fo is more of a Gramscian than he is a Marxist. He often refers to Gramsci in relation to the lessons of history. But since Gramsci never calls for a refashioning of facts or of history, the answers as to why Fo took this course might better be explained on the basis his personal interpretations of Gramscian social philosophy. Although it may be impossible to determine for certain why Fo made certain artistic decisions, the fact remains that the re-presentation of history became an integral part of his theatre. Over time, as Fo drew more and more from carnival culture (the subject of the following chapter), his playing with facts became a sort of performance prank, used to make a point. Chapter 3 is primarily concerned with how Fo re-presents history in order to undermine the hegemony of official culture while validating and giving dignity to folk culture. It also explores which historical periods he favors and why he favors them. Together these functions of history constitute important elements in the overriding thematic frame that defines his theatre.

While temporarily setting aside direct reference to Fo's theatre, chapter 4 is dedicated entirely to historical and anthropological background of the European carnival, essential to the analyses of the final chapters. The carnival with its satirical and Saturnalian elements is central to Fo's hegemonic worldview. It is an extensive topic, and the investigation must perforce be limited to those aspects that are most pertinent to his theatre. Although Fo's interest in carnival culture predates the publication of *Rabelais and His World* in Western Europe in 1968, Mikhail Bakhtin's hallmark work was a great influence on him. Since I have dealt extensively with the Bakhtinian aspects of Fo's work in *Dario Fo and Popular Performance*, mention of Bakhtin has been intentionally limited. Instead, this chapter will focus on another work on the carnival which had a great impact on Fo: *Le origini del teatro italiano* (The origins of Italian theatre) by anthropologist Paolo Toschi. This lengthy book traces the prehistoric origins of the European carnival, follows their survival in various local Italian traditions, and demonstrates their influence on folk performance, medieval mystery plays, and the *commedia dell'arte*. Toschi's study is complemented by the more theoretical works on ritual symbolism by his younger contemporary, Victor Turner. Both anthropologists were interested in links between ritual and theatre, and both were heavily influenced by the hallmark work on the rites of passage by Arnold Van Gennep. Turner develops Van Gennep's concept of liminality in ritual, whereby social and cosmic orders are temporarily suspended. Over time, as a ritual loses its original import, elements of liminality are passed on in different forms. Turner describes these vestiges of liminality as *liminoid*. The process helps to explain how the European carnival transformed over the millennia.

Thus chapter 4 traces carnivalesque elements as they continued in the Middle Ages. The satirical aspects of carnival and carnivalesque elements in medieval society explain Fo's interest in this historical period, discussed in the previous chapter. During the medieval and Renaissance periods, the carnival became a symbol of tension between the popular culture of the masses and the official culture of the nobility. The period of liminality gave the peasantry leave to mock the authorities and the upper classes. The Roman Church viewed the carnival as a survival of the pagan culture it intended to supplant. The tension between Church and carnival was a salient aspect of the struggle between official and popular cultures (as Bakhtin so cogently argued). Although the carnival lost its original meaning as an agrarian rite, during the Christian era the spirit of the carnival continued in myriad forms of celebration that brought together spectacle and satire. One of the most important *liminoid* vestiges of the carnival was the figure of the *giullare*, who took on some of the liminal elements of the Lord of Misrule, the central symbol of Italian carnival celebrations. The medieval *giullare* was in essence a *fool*, with that special brand of madness that allowed him to speak the truth and criticize others, even his betters. This quality of the fool continued in the Renaissance (such as in Shakespeare's fools) and survives as a *liminoid* icon in the joker of English playing cards. All of this helps to explain why so many of

Fo's plays take place during Middle Ages and Renaissance, why the *giullare* is so important to him, and how an overriding carnival frame works in his theatre.

Chapter 5 looks at how Fo established the principles of the carnival and carnivalesque vestiges as an overriding frame of his theatre. This began in the 1960s with two important works: *Isabella, Three Sailing Ships and a Conman* (1966) and *Mistero buffo* (1977b) (the latter being Fo's first *giullarata*). These plays initiated the conscious process of creating a carnival frame, and Fo began to identify himself with the Lord of Misrule and the *giullare*. As the Lord of Misrule, Fo allows himself to suspend social structure and the order that generally defines our notions of reality. Contextualized within the Saturnalian misrule of the carnival, the mixing of fact and fiction and the re-presentation of history are given a sense of justification as part of the performance. The carnival frame works in Fo's theatre at a deeper level as well. The prehistoric carnival rituals were marked by a grotesque combination of human and animal features that were displayed in the zoomorphic masks that accompanied the celebrations and continued in the masks of the commedia dell'arte. In Fo's theatre, zoomorphic symbolism becomes an important element and works in various ways. This chapter ends with special focus on the mythological aspects of his *giullarata* "The Tale of a Tiger" (the principal sketch of *The Tale of a Tiger and Other Stories*) (1980). "Tiger" was first produced in 1979, and given Fo's age, it is not surprising that his understanding of myth was influenced by the works of certain scholars of his day, such as Carl Gustav Jung and Claude Levi-Strauss. The latter's study on Amazonian fire-theft myths is central to understanding Fo's tale.

The final chapter brings together all of the discussions on performance framing, history, and anthropology of the previous chapters in a focused analysis of one play. It is dedicated entirely to another mature work, *The Holy Jester Francis* (1999a), and to its central figure, Saint Francis of Assisi. This *giullarata* premiered in 1999 at The Festival of the Two Worlds in Spoleto. Fo bases his portrayal of Saint Francis on certain historical realities. There is much evidence to sustain that the historical Francis used performance, specifically in the register of the *giullare,* as his primary means of communicating his exempla. And like other figures in mystical traditions of the past, Francis exhibited qualities of the enlightened *fool*. By clever framing and by reference to his indexical frame, Fo manages to re-present Francis as a Fo-*giullare*, in a carnivalesque and satirical register, without falling into gross parody or even offending the Catholic Church. Fo's Francis validates the culture of the downtrodden, while criticizing the abuse of power by the elite. He also uses Francis' legendary mystical rapport with animals to inform the play with an element of pre-Christian totemic mythology. Besides original accounts and biographies, several historical works on Saint Francis are central to this chapter, including one by Chiara Frugoni, which Fo used in preparing the play.

As would be expected, after being awarded the Nobel Prize for Literature in 1997, Fo's theatre has garnered more scholarly attention, including doctoral dissertations, articles, and books. This increased activity is most welcomed and greatly enriches the field. Several sourcebooks and biographical works (cited throughout this book) facilitated the research for this project. These and other studies that approach the topic from different angles and focus on other aspects of Fo—such as his politics and/or the various phases of his career—provided useful insight and information. The present study looks at Fo's theatre from an interdisciplinary perspective, with the intention of providing a better understanding of the interrelationship of various techniques and mechanisms involving framing, festival, and the folkloric imagination.

Notes

1. These performers, all of whom acknowledge the importance of Fo's *giullarata* as fundamental to their careers, include Marco Baliani, Laura Curino, Marco Polini, and Davide Enia. See Soriani 2009.

2. For more on Fo's art, see Cairns 2000. Occasionally Fo also composes songs for his plays (although not his strongest skill). See Mitchell 2000.

3. Rame and Fo 2009 is an autobiographical work. Other works on Franca Rame include, Wood 2000, Valeri 2000, and D'Arcangeli 2009.

Chapter Two

Metacommunication and the Interpretive Frame

Framing in Folklore Studies

Throughout this study the analytic device known as *framing*, which began with the social sciences, will be used in order to gain greater insight into Dario Fo's theatre. Gregory Bateson is generally accredited as the first social scientist to formulate frame as a concept in cognitive studies, in his essay "A Theory of Play and Fantasy" (1972:177-93).[1] Erving Goffman further developed it in his hallmark book, *Frame Analysis*, where he conceives frames as cognitive processes that help shape the perception and organization of reality: "I assume that definitions of a situation are built up in accordance with principles of organization which govern events—at least social ones—and our subjective involvement with them; frame is the word I use to refer to such of these basic elements as I am able to identify. That is my definition of frame" (1986:10-11).

Collectively frames assist in communication and social interaction. *Keying* is the process by which individuals define a frame and give structure to their interactions. Borrowing the term from music, Goffman considers the concept of a "key change" as shifting, transposing, or even canceling a key, thus changing the frame. "I refer here to the set of conventions by which a given activity, one already meaningful in terms of some primary framework, is transformed into something patterned on this activity but seen by the participants to be something quite else. The process of transcription can be called keying" (1986:43-44).

Goffman dedicates a chapter to "The Theatrical Frame." His definition of performance "in the restricted sense" is limited to conventional, formal performances. It requires that "a line is ordinarily maintained between a staging area where the performance proper occurs and an audience region where the watchers are located" (1986:124-25), that invisible barrier known as "the fourth wall." His definition also requires "the central understanding . . . that the audience has neither the right nor the obligation to participate directly in the dramatic action occurring on the stage" (1986:125).[2] In a note, Goffman draws a distinction between his definition and "a different definition" (1986:124, n.1), proposed by the linguistic anthropologist Dell Hymes, who uses an expanded notion of performance that includes certain human behavior and activities that may occur outside formal settings.[3]

It is this expanded concept of performance which Richard Bauman takes up and expounds in his seminal work, *Verbal Art as Performance*.[4] Drawing from various ethnographic studies, as well as theoretical studies from various fields, Bauman works with a definition of performance that goes beyond conventional settings and "artful texts": "Performance involves on the part of the performer an assumption of accountability to an audience for the way in which communication is carried out, above and beyond its referential content" (1984:11). "It is part of the essence of performance that it offers to the participants a special enhancement of experience, bringing with it a heightened intensity of communicative interaction which binds the audience to the performer in a way that is specific to performance as a mode of communication" (1984:43). Based on ethnographic evidence, Bauman makes the point that in some cultural contexts the situation is more complex than simply identifying a frame as performance or nonperformance. In such contexts, performance may be perceived as functioning at various levels, and "the performance frame may thus be seen to operate with variable intensity..." (1984:23-24).[5]

Other issues that Bauman addresses include how possibilities for keying in a performance frame may vary in different communities and in different situations. "In empirical terms, this means that each speech community will make use of a structural set of distinctive communicative means from among its resources in culturally conventionalized and culture-specific ways to key the performance frame..." (1984:16). In the context of folklore and anthropology, it is essential to address the cultural conventions that determine how and when a performance can be keyed. Bauman identifies some of the more prevalent techniques that have been documented in various cultures. These include special codes, figurative language, parallelism, special paralinguistic features, special formulae, appeal to tradition, and disclaimer of performance (1984:16-

24). The various possibilities for keying in a performance, along with the various levels of intensity a performance may take, are all contributing factors that give most popular, oral performances some degree of emergent and protean qualities. For example, less formal performances, such as stories and jokes, may be keyed in at any time, as long as the moment and situation seem appropriate. And in formal settings, many traditions allow for spontaneous modifications of both the narrative content and the duration. Drawing from the important work of Milman Parry and Albert Lord on the Serbo-Croatian epic-ballad singers, called *guslari* (Lord 1960), Bauman explains, "the point is that completely novel and completely fixed texts represent the poles of an ideal continuum, and that between the poles lies the range of emergent text structures to be found in empirical performance" (1984:40).

Metacommunicative possibilities were an inherent part of Bateson's original concept of frame: "Any message, which either explicitly or implicitly defines a frame, *ipso facto* gives the receiver instructions or aids in his attempt to understand the messages included within the frame" (1972:188). In verbal performance metanarration can be a powerful communicative tool.

> By focusing our attention on the act or process of communicating, such devices lead us away from and back to the message by supplying a "frame," an interpretive context or alternative point of view within which the content of the story is to be understood and judged. . . . Within the external frame of the performance, specific reference is often made to the performer, the audience, the message, the code, the channel or medium of expression, the register, etc., or to any combination thereof. (Babcock 1984:66-67)

In his studies on traditional oral narrative, John Miles Foley also draws on the work of Parry and Lord. Important to this study is his discussion of how the interpretation of an oral performance that is part of a living tradition remains, to some degree, open to the individual receiver, while at the same time maintaining a certain degree of homogeneity that is shared by all receivers. It is the tradition itself that provides the homogeneous quality and encodes the frame with indexical meaning that goes beyond the literal level.

An essential part of this process is the concept of *immanence* in verbal art. "For the record, immanence may be defined as the set of metonymic, associative meanings institutionally delivered and received through a dedicated idiom or register either during or on the authority of the traditional oral performer" (Foley 1995:7). Words or units of utterance, within the frame, are informed with special extratextual significance that is understood within the tradition. "That is, the traditional phrase or scene or story-pattern has an indexical meaning vis-à-vis the immanent tradition; each integer reaches beyond the confines of the individual performance or oral-derived text to a set of traditional ideas much larger and richer than any single performance or text" (1995:6).[6] This encompasses many aspects of a given storytelling tradition, such as the epithet in the epic tradition, whereby "'grey-eyed Athena' would serve as an approved traditional channel or pathway for summoning the Athena not just of this or that particular moment, but rather of all moments in the experience of audience and poet." The epithet stands metonymically "for the character in all of his or her traditional complexity" (1995:5). Likewise other special phrases, such as the *guslar*'s "well-wrought tower" or Homer's "wine-dark sea," "act as prompts, invoking a context in which the audience is to construe the poet's words" (Foley 2002:90).

Framing in Fo's Theatre

Applying some of these principles of folklore performance studies to Dario Fo provides great insight into his craft and genius and into the workings of his theatre as an organic entity. He is very aware of the differences between the keying of performance in a formal theatrical play and in popular traditions. Simply put in his own words: "The absence of the opening of the curtain is the greatest tradition belonging to all popular theatre" (1978). By "opening of the curtain," he intends those conventional signals (including the lowering of the house lights) that markedly key in the performance frame. Borrowing various techniques from Italian variety theatre of the past, he creates a gradual keying, playing with the notion that various levels of performance operate with variable intensity. He is often present on stage as people are entering the theatre and finding their seats, sometimes joking about who is sitting where and whose husband is home watching the game. He refers to this as his *anteprologo* (1987:164; 1992a:97). By being present on stage, he attempts to diminish or remove the sense of a fourth wall, the imaginary line between audience and performer that was essential to Goffman's formal definition. Thus he begins a gradual keying towards the performance frame.

The *anteprologo* is important but not essential. When the house is full, however, he begins his trademark extended prologue or *discorsetto* (little speech), which does represent an essential part of his framing. The prologue calls for the audience's attention, but is relaxed and chatty, thus at a lower intensity level than the performance proper. And by means of his extended prologue, Fo establishes an interpretive frame for each performance (whether farce and *giullarata*). Mixing fact with a good dose of fiction, he directly addresses the audience and provides a background to what they are about to see. The prologue generally includes historical events, current events, Fo's research into the subject, personal anecdotes, and the like. In the process he suggests to the audience how they should interpret the performance and lays out the historical and/or sociopolitical points he intends to convey. As will be discussed, this in turn is enhanced by the overall indexical, interpretive frame of his theatre.

The gradual keying establishes a "flexible frame"[7] that allows Fo to weave in and out of character for metatheatrical purposes. At any given moment during a show, Fo and/or Franca Rame will break character and address the audience or one another as themselves. This sort of break may be either spontaneous or indicated in the written text. In an essay entitled "*Amphitruo, Bacchae,* and Metatheatre," Niall Slater defines metatheatre as, "theatrically self-conscious theatre, aware of its own nature as a medium and capable of exploiting its own conventions and devices for comic and occasionally pathetic effect" (2001:189). Certainly metatheatre has a long history and was expertly exploited by Plautus in his plays for comic effect. But with Fo its function is primarily metacommunicative, often adverting to his established interpretive frame. During the performance he uses metatheatric techniques primarily in two ways: specifically to underscore a point and in general to remind the audience of the performance frame. Frequent references to the performance itself help shift attention to its messages. Following the tenets of epic theatre, Fo intends for his plays to avoid emotional catharsis and move audiences to consider their messages, with the result of urging them towards social and political action. Although he originally derived the concept of epic theatre from Brecht, Fo soon realized that many of its principles, including the lack of the fourth wall, were present in ancient theatre and in various forms of popular performance.[8] The methods Fo utilizes for breaking the fourth wall in his farces are taken mostly from variety theatre and are akin to forms of classical theatre and the commedia dell'arte.

In his book *Immanent Art*, Foley discusses the difference between *inherent* meaning, which is more prominent in traditional contexts, as opposed to meaning that is *conferred* on a modern narrative by the author. "A traditional work depends primarily on elements and strategies that were in place long before the execution of the present version or text . . ." (1991:8). Unlike traditional performers around the world, Fo is not working within a living oral tradition with an ancient and well-defined indexical frame. Although he is conferring meaning to his works, he is nonetheless aware of the concept of an overriding thematic frame that can be developed by an individual performer. In the opening of his book on the Neapolitan vaudevillian and film star Totò (Antonio De Curtis, 1898-1967), he discusses an actor's *poetics*, i.e. his/her trademark idiom and style. "Totò has poetics that is rich in *themes and motifs that weave and dovetail, presenting a whole and complex vision* that is always identifiable as being Totò's" (1991a:9, emphasis added). Fo has intentionally repeated certain themes, motifs, and strategies across his performances, over time creating a greater organic frame of interlocking, associative themes. The result is a mechanism akin to what Foley describes in traditional oral narrative: An element contextualized in a performance may be informed with extratextual, indexical meaning that "reaches beyond the confines of the individual performance" (1995:6).

As one might expect, Fo's thematic frame is much richer and more extensive at home. To begin with, the vast majority of his plays are in standard Italian and are thus more immediate to Italian audiences. There are also numerous plays that, for various reasons, have had a limited life outside of Italy. Some are simply less successful, while others seem to have a more restricted, national appeal.[9] In Italy the network of interlocking themes is expanded, reinforced, and enriched by Fo's many activities. (This is also true, although to a lesser extent, in Europe, where he garners a respectable degree of popularity.) These include television appearances, articles, books, paintings, statements to the press, and even public acts of defiance to authorities.[10] However, although Fo's thematic frame is more effective within its Italian context, it paradoxically contributes to his wider popularity around the world, as will be discussed below.

Thus Fo's distinctive use of framing entails, first of all, his establishing a flexible performance frame. The prologue, as a low-intensity performance, works as a transition between non-performance and performance frames. It simultaneously defines the interpretive frame by laying out the issues that the play will be addressing. In the prologue as well as in the performance, he repeats a host of themes and motifs found in his other works, connecting the play to a greater indexical or thematic frame. The flexible frame allows him to refer to the issues established in the prologue and the related themes of his indexical frame. And "By focusing our attention on the act or process of communicating," he constantly shifts the focus away from the performance to the messages. This will be illustrated in the following analysis of a later play and its relationship to the greater indexical frame.

Frame Analysis of *The Two-Headed Anomaly*

One of Fo's most quoted statements is his assertion that "Our theatre is a throwaway theatre [*teatro da bruciare*], a theatre which won't go down in bourgeois history, but which is useful, like a newspaper article, a debate or a political action" (Mitchell 1999:101).[11] Although scholars may disagree about the extent to which this is true, it nevertheless calls attention to a defining quality of his theatre. Whereas his one-man shows (*giullarate*), such as

Mistero buffo and *Johan Padan*, are well thought out and well constructed performance pieces, many of his satirical farces, which constitute the bulk of his opus, are not. They are often put together quickly in order to address current events. All of Fo's works, including the *giullarate*, represent flexible texts that are open to improvisations and other changes, giving them an emergent quality that is reminiscent of traditional performance. The satirical farces in particular are often modified, from one show to the next, to incorporate current events as they occur. Perhaps the best example is *Accidental Death of an Anarchist*, which evolved as a related trial was taking place. The trial was a lawsuit against the leftist newspaper, *Lotta Continua*. "The play was constantly updated, each performance including reports on the day's hearing in the *Lotta Continua* case" (Mitchell 1999:103). This approach puts the focus of the performance on communicating a message and making a point at the expense of the craft that typically defines the conventional sense of "good theatre."

In December of 2003, Dario Fo and Franca Rame debuted *The Two-Headed Anomaly* (*L'Anomalo bicefalo*), a satire aimed primarily at Italian Prime Minister Silvio Berlusconi.[12] *The Two-Headed Anomaly* is very much a throw-away theatrical piece, designed to address specific issues in a specific time and place. It also represents a culmination of Fo's brand of epic theatre, which draws on farcical metatheatric techniques from vaudeville and clowning.

The title refers to the farcical and surrealistic premise of the play, in which a piece of Russian President Vladamir Putin's brain is transplanted into Silvio Berlusconi's head in an emergency operation. Fo portrays Berlusconi as an evil dwarf, employing the same vaudeville gag he used to lampoon former Italian prime minister Amintore Fanfani in *Fanfani Kidnapped* (the dwarf gag is described below). The play directs satirical criticism at Berlusconi's flagrant abuse of power and his conflicts of interest as owner of a media empire, which includes three out of the seven national television channels. (Another three out of the seven national channels are run by the government.) A review published in the *New York Times* suggests that "for all of its grave accusations, the *Two-Headed Anomaly* is an almost vaudevillian romp. The show consists largely of short, fat and bald jokes about the prime minister and his councilors. It stages attacks not only on Mr. Berlusconi's politics but also his personal life and his ethics" (Horowitz 2003:B1, B16). Despite the nasty digs, in particular the references to Berlusconi's stature, Fo's intention is to go beyond silly, below-the-belt lampooning. He claims that he originally went into theatre "with the aspiration of playing the clown, the buffoon, but seriously" (1987:112). At an immediate level, *Anomaly* is certainly a throw-away piece and a romp, put together quickly and based on absurdly farcical premises. A closer look however reveals an intricate play of performance frames and character dynamics. The constant shift of frames and the metacommunicative devices are at the service of an interpretive frame that is established in the prologue and supported by the greater thematic frame.

Since the metacommunicative devices are meant to "lead us away from and back to the message[s]" that are established primarily by the prologue, it is essential that the interpretive frame be addressed. The prologue, presented as an informal chat, is not delivered as a scripted piece. Thus the prologues of the versions used for this study present some variations, but the primary points are essentially the same[13] (for *Anomaly* it was sometimes delivered by Franca Rame). The prologue may be summarized as follows: Fo and Rame were ready to take a long rest and spend some time seeing their plays performed abroad. But with the outrageous events happening around the world, such as the second war in Iraq and Berlusconi's antics in Italy, they could not remain idle and quickly threw together this satire. Fo describes what he claims was an early version of the play, and how real events became so unbelievable that they made the original premise look less like farce and more like reality. They realized that in order to keep the register of the play more farcical than reality, they had to come up with something truly outrageous. He explains that, despite their attempts, "The facts in our political world were copying everything we invented" (2004b), and he suggests that politicians were stealing their ideas for the play. He explains how various powerful people attempted to block both the production of the play and TV broadcast. Others threatened lawsuits. These are presented as attempts to censor the play that were successfully thwarted by counteractions, which consisted mostly in drumming up bad publicity. "When you react in the face of intimidation, you always win" (2004b).[14] As Fo has often done in the past, he expounds on the subversive nature of satire and how it is a tool for turning a situation on its head, revealing infamy and hypocrisy and getting to the truth. He explains that it is "an extraordinary instrument that existed since the beginning of time, just think of Aristophanes and the *giullari* of the Middle Ages" (2004a:7).

The primary points that the prologue lays out therefore are as follows:

- No matter how hopeless a situation seems to be, we must never remain inactive.
- The true farce is not the play but rather the outrageous lies, corruption, and abuses of those in power.
- Grotesque satire is a powerful weapon that threatens the mighty.
- The previous points have been demonstrated and substantiated by the course of events: Fo and Rame decided not to sit idly, and with this satire they have made their contribution, albeit minimal.

The satire had an effect on its targets, i.e. corrupt politicians who tried to censure the play. But by staying the course and with help from other good people, Fo and Rame overcame the obstacles. These, along with the criticism leveled at Berlusconi and other politicians, are the messages Fo wishes to be conveyed and underscored by the performance.

Much of the highlighting and underscoring is accomplished through metacommunicative devices that refer back to the interpretive frame established by the prologue. The play thus opens with the screen test of an actress (Rame) reading from Aristophanes' *Lysistrata* (actually, a paraphrase). Lysistrata is calling the women of Athens to action, and in the process she alludes to some of the primary points of the prologue: "We can't continue like this, so faint-hearted and resigned. Women! Women! We have a powerful and invincible weapon, and we must put it in the field" (2004b). Thus the opening lines situate the play in the tradition of early satirical comedies such as those of Aristophanes, warn of the consequences of resignation and inaction, and make their own call to action.

The play is essentially a two-person show, with Fo and Rame playing the leads. There are two walk-on characters who bring in props and deliver an occasional line, and a mime who stands behind Fo and whose hands become those of the Berlusconi dwarf. (To execute the dwarf gag, Fo's legs are concealed, and his arms and hands, fitted with tiny pants and shoes, become the dwarf's legs and feet.) Anastasia (Rame) is an actress who has been engaged for a good amount of money to play a role in a film. She is now meeting for the first time with the director of the film (played by Fo) in his studio to read through the script that she is seeing for the first time. She soon learns that the film will be a scathing satire on Berlusconi. The Director informs her that all of the actors who had agreed to play the other roles backed out when they discovered the nature of film, presumably for fear of repercussions. Therefore he must play all of the other characters in this read-through.

It is later revealed that Anastasia is an ex-communist who abandoned the party out of disgust for their inaction (and because they kept changing their name) (44). She is now a staunch conservative and a great admirer of Berlusconi. But because she is in financial straits, due to bad investments, such as Parmalat (43),[15] and because she has already spent her generous advance, she is willing to play the role. She tries to conceal her conservative side until she can no longer stand it. At the moment of the revelation, Anastasia's tone completely changes. The function of this twist will be discussed below.

On various occasions Fo has stated that he is first and foremost a storyteller (1992a:69). This certainly holds true for his *giullarata*, which is primarily a storytelling event. It also has to do with the concept in epic theatre that the story overrides characters in importance. As it is structured, *The Two-Headed Anomaly* primarily utilizes narrative. We learn of the farcical situation that is the premise for the film as the Director narrates it to Anastasia: Putin and Berlusconi are staying in the latter's villa in Sicily while a conference of transplant surgeons is taking place nearby. They are attacked by Chechen terrorists, Putin is killed, and Berlusconi is badly

20   Chapter Two

wounded. The surgeons save Berlusconi by removing the damaged part of his brain and replacing it with part of Putin's.

Anastasia reads the part of Veronica Lario, who was Berlusconi's wife at the time. The Director plays several roles: a Russian surgeon (Surgeon) who explains more details about Silvio's condition; the tutor for the Berlusconis' children (Tutor), a friend of the family, to whom Veronica explains aspects of Silvio's bizarre behavior; and Silvio. A good part of the read-through entails Veronica sitting with Silvio (Fo) and narrating his past to him, since he has lost much of his memory (near the end, Anastasia briefly plays a Berlusconi spokesperson as well).

The play is a metanarrational series of Chinese boxes. There is a frame story of Anastasia and the Director reading through the script of the Director's film, which creates a play within a play. At the end, a Wizard-of-Oz-like voice comes over the PA system and announces that *he* is the true director (the Director is really only an actor), and that this has all been part of *his* movie. During the performance there are plenty of Fo and Rame's usual metatheatric breaks of character, both scripted and improvised. The two primary actors move in and out of various characters as well as breaking character and being themselves. In summary, the personae/characters the two main actors portray are as follows:

- Dario Fo plays the Director, who plays the Tutor, the Surgeon, and Silvio Berlusconi
- Franca Rame plays Anastasia, who plays Veronica and a Spokesperson

Thus, with stage directions such as, "getting out of character," "getting back into character," Rame moves from Veronica to Anastasia back to Veronica; and Fo moves from Silvio, the Tutor, or the Surgeon, to the Director and back. They also move from any of these characters to Franca and Dario. At some points, for example, Rame's character is referred to in the directions as Anastasia-Veronica and Fo's as Director-Silvio, and at one point even Franca-Anastasia-Veronica and Dario-Director-Silvio (57). This Chinese-box structure, of a play within a play, allows for the two principal actors to shift in and out of several characters as well as their own personae.

It has been established that the ultimate goal of this type of performance is to highlight its socio-political messages. Fo's epic-theatre approach rejects Stanislavskian concepts of theatre, in which the actor attempts to get into character at a psychological level and to perform as if the audience were not there. Specifically in *Anomaly*, the constant shifting in and out of character and in and out of the frame-story creates innumerable metatheatric breaks, whereby the audience is reminded of the performance frame. This prevents them from getting involved with the characters and keeps them focused on the story and its messages. The various combinations of characters interacting also set up different tones and registers that communicate different things to the audience in different ways. For this discussion of *Anomaly*, specifically with reference to the dialogue between characters, *register* is used in its restricted linguistic sense, that is, a functional variety of a language appropriate to a given speech situation, as determined by social setting, the social status of the users and the degree of formality between them, and the topic(s) being discussed.[16] These are the primary combinations of the characters:

Anastasia (actress)/Director
Veronica/Surgeon
Veronica/Tutor
Veronica/Silvio
Anastasia (right-wing conservative)/Director

Anastasia (actress) and the Director converse in the cordial, professional register of employee and employer, underscored by the use of the formal direct-address (*lei*). The Director explains his reasons for making a scathing satire on Berlusconi. Anastasia politely listens, adds some reasons of her own, and lists the sins of Putin as well. The primary function of their exchanges is to inform the audience of the plot of the film. As they move from the frame story to the read-through, Veronica first interacts with the Surgeon. This is also in a formal register and serves primarily to inform the audience of Silvio Berlusconi's condition and what Veronica needs to do to help him recover. Almost immediately they break character, as Anastasia tries to read a line with the proper emotion, moving back and forth between frame story and read-through.

When the Director calls for a scene change and explains to Anastasia who the Tutor is, he defines the register: "I will be your children's tutor, a good friend you regard highly" (2004b). They get into character and in their conversation, in which they use the familiar address (*tu*), Veronica tells the Tutor about Silvio's bizarre behavior since his accident. She explains that Silvio will occasionally and unexpectedly break into a strange language, and proceeds to rattle off some Slavic *grammelot* (the theatrical technique of pretending to speak by simulating its sounds, cadence, and intonation).[17]

> Tutor: What a strange language? But what does the doctor who's caring for him have to say?
>
> Anastasia: (*Getting out of character*) The doctor? He was just here in the last scene! (*She and Dario Laugh as audience applauds*) (2004b)

This is the same sort of simple metatheatric break we find, for example, in ancient Roman comedy, whereby an actor refers to the performance. But here it is working on three levels: Rame is playing Anastasia (in the frame story), who is playing Veronica (in the film read-through). In this instance she is referring to the performance within the performance. This and the other examples that do not refer to a specific message serve nevertheless to keep the audience from getting involved emotionally with the characters.

Shortly afterwards it is Fo's turn. Although the Silvio character is the most clown-like, the Fo clown can break through at any moment, as it does when an allusion is made to Jekyll and Hyde. The Tutor, who up to this point has been expressing sincere concern, begins to emit feral sounds as he mimes a sort of werewolf (2004b). Should an audience member begin to feel an inkling of pathos for the characters, the clown destroys any possibility by breaking the flow. In fact the constant meta-breaks never let the play settle into a flow of any sort.

Although to some extent satire permeates the entire play, thus far the three combinations of characters examined (Director/Anastasia, Veronica/Surgeon, Veronica/Tutor) have functioned primarily to set up the central theme of the play, which comes with the entrée of the Silvio-clown. By means of the conversations of the three sets of characters, the audience is made aware of the situation that necessitated the brain exchange. The audience also knows that Veronica was lied to, and that she believes Silvio's condition is the result of an accident, in which he fell down a flight of stairs, bumping his head forty-something times. They know that in order to help him recover, she has been advised to reconcile with him and try to take him back in. Most importantly, they know that she must fill him in on his past, since he has lost a good deal of his memory.

The Silvio dwarf enters with a ridiculous dance, accompanied by Carpi's vaudevillian music. After a brief civil exchange, Veronica proceeds to admonish him sternly for being a "pathological liar" (33) and for all his dishonesty, in their personal lives, in politics, and in business. She reminds him of all of his antics, which he seems to have forgotten. She assumes an angry tone of indignation, and it carries over into a metatheatric break. As she is berating Silvio for the fraudulent financial maneuvers that have made him a billionaire, she states, "Listen up Silvio . . . (*to the audience*) and you listen up as well, there is nothing fabricated here . . ." (34).What follows are allegations (facts, according to Fo and Rame) about Berlusconi's fraudulent businesses, tax shelters, etc.

Silvio however reacts with a "Who me?" attitude, cracking jokes, showing no remorse, nor acknowledging the gravity of what he has done. On the contrary, he is quite pleased with himself:

Director-Silvio: They convicted me? For false testimony?

Anastasia-Veronica: Of course! You were guilty! But a pardon arrived and you saved yourself at the last minute, as you always do!

Director-Silvio: What ass![18] Oh, I'm enjoying this immensely! (2004b)

The dynamics of Veronica and Silvio hark back to the comic opposition of Roman clowns, and of the first and second *zanni* of the commedia dell'arte. More precisely, the dynamics of the two characters correspond to a later manifestation of this formula, namely the authoritative White Clown and the subaltern August of the early circus.[19] Rame plays the "straight man," but Fo adds another dimension by playing his part as a *sot* or fool. In the grotesque medieval comedies known as *soties*, everyone from peasants to authority figures, including kings and popes, were portrayed as fools.[20] Fo uses the *sot* device to undermine Berlusconi's authority and credibility.

In clown mode, Silvio directs some stinging criticism at the public. "What a swindle! God! Oh God! (*Laughs, delighted*) And there are still assholes, millions of assholes that continue to vote for me!" (37). Then in the second act there is criticism directed at the low-grade nature of television programming, and Silvio, the broadcasting mogul, takes a nasty shot at television viewers:

Director-Silvio: (...) do you know that insect, a type of beetle that lives in the desert and eats only excrement?

Anastasia-Veronica: Of course, the dung-beetle.

Director-Silvio: Precisely. To keep the dung-beetle happy, you must perforce feed him shit. (53)

At a certain point Anastasia has an unexpected outburst. She proclaims that she is being forced to go against all of her principles and that she is actually a great admirer of Silvio Berlusconi. This changes the dynamics as well as the register drastically. The niceties that earlier marked the Anastasia (actress)/Director rapport are dropped, and the tone and register become confrontational. Like the Veronica/Silvio situation above, Rame continues to play the authoritative White Clown. However, now she sings the praises of Berlusconi, while Fo (no longer the Silvio *sot*) undermines her with classic clown antics. As she denounces the outrage of the satire and proclaims the positive qualities of Berlusconi, the Fo clown subverts her assertions:

Anastasia: I'm a Berlusconian! I'm a Berlusconian! And thank God there is a man of his strength, of his courage, who saved our country!

Director: Of his stature! Moral stature, that is. (2004b)[21]

An interesting *lazzo*, reminiscent of early circus clowning, occurs when Anastasia complains about depicting Berlusconi with two heads.

Director: Look, if I were him I'd think about this idea of the two heads, two brains! One to make declarations and the other to deny them immediately! (*He mimes pressing two brains into one and playing with it like a ball*)

Anastasia: Stop it! Give me that ball! (*The Director pretends to pass the ball to her, and she pretends to throw it to the audience*) And don't you dare throw it back to him. (42)

On several occasions Fo has discussed the technique of the "accident" in this type of performance, that is, having the actors pretend that something has gone wrong. In other words, they pretend that the performance frame has been keyed out, when in fact the staged accident continues to be in the performance frame. He has used this technique effectively various times.[22] In the text of *Anomaly*, as the Director and Anastasia are arguing, Franca Rame pretends to have misspoken. She says "*spuzzolentare*," a word that does not exist in Italian. This provides the opportunity for one of the most extended metatheatric breaks of the play:[23] Fo comes out of character and proclaims, "I didn't write that bit! *Spuzzolentare!*" Then Rame comes out of character, laughing too hard to respond. Fo addresses the audience, "But who gave the Nobel to the guy who says *Spuzzolentare!*" They carry on: Fo continuing to make fun of the invented word, and Rame trying to make him stop and reprimanding the audience for laughing at his shenanigans. She uses this opportunity to tell them how many years she has put up with him, as his collaborator and as his spouse (2004b).

They get back into character, and their argument echoes the prologue: specifically the attempts to prevent *Anomaly* from being broadcast. Anastasia reminds the Director that it will be virtually impossible for him to distribute his film, since Berlusconi owns the major distribution companies. Then the issue of action versus inaction that was laid out in the prologue is addressed. Anastasia, who revealed that she had been a communist, directs criticism at the Italian left. In a sudden volte-face, she admits that she is disgusted with the illegal activities and the conflict of interests of those presently in power. The fault however lies with the left for their inertia. They controlled the government for five years, yet they never put into place antitrust laws. She implies that she is more disgusted with the inactivity of the left than with the criminal activities of the right.

Representing Authority

In *Anomaly* the portrayal of Berlusconi as a mutilated dwarf, with half of Vladimir Putin's brain comes charged with indexical import. This parody of an authority figure is informed by the greater thematic frame that reaches beyond the confines of the immediate performance. Fo used the same dwarf gag in the 1970s to play one of Italy's most powerful political figures in *Fanfani Kidnapped*. Amintore Fanfani was one of the founding fathers of the Italian Christian Democratic party and served as prime minister six times. *Fanfani Kidnapped* has been described as an "off-the-cuff, rough-and-ready burlesque" (Farrell 2001:152), which parallels Horowitz's assessment of *Anomaly* as a "vaudevillian romp" and suggests similarities between the two plays. But like *Anomaly*, *Fanfani* was intended to convey something beyond its immediate political satire and zany slapstick, as Fo himself expressed: "[it] is not cabaret, nor is it a satire of a famous member of the government and his mannerisms and weaknesses. *It is a grotesque representation of authority* . . ." (emphasis added).[24] This is an important theme that defines Fo's greater indexical frame, which in turn helps to support and define the interpretive frame of each performance.

In *Fanfani* the grotesque elements of the representation run wild, starting with Fanfani being kidnapped and wetting himself from fright. When the kidnappers cut off one of his ears, for anesthesia they have him drink *sambuca*, the sweet, anise-flavored liqueur. Lacking alcohol, they use a glass of *sambuca* to preserve the ear, resulting in a "candied ear" (1976:37). They then dress him up like a woman and bring him to an abortion clinic. The trauma of being kidnapped causes his sphincter to close shut, while the great quantity of *sambuca* he drank creates tremendous amounts of gas, which causes his belly to swell, as if he were pregnant. In a lowbrow gag, the audience is led to believe that the exaggerated flatulent noises they hear are coming from Fanfani, only to learn that there is a leaky pipe in the building. The gas in Fanfani is released by inserting an enormous "Chinese suppository" that also happens to cause grotesque nightmares. As he is relieved of the gas, while simultaneously hallucinating, he "gives birth" to a son—an allegorical puppet that represents fascism.[25] Like the multi-layered frame of *Anomaly*, it turns out Fanfani dreamt his kidnapping. Thus the grotesque nightmare, which takes him all the way to the afterlife, was a dream within a dream.

In one of Fo's most famous plays, *Accidental Death of an Anarchist*, police headquarters in Milan is infiltrated by a zany lunatic, referred to as "il Matto" (madman or *sot*), originally played by Fo. At one point the fool disguises himself as a captain of police forensics. His disguise consists of an eye patch, a wooden arm, and a wooden leg. Perhaps as an allegorical dismantling of official power and authority, he systematically comes apart. A congratulatory slap on the back knocks out his glass eye, his wooden arm comes off in a handshake and is replaced by that of a female mannequin. A grotesque representation of power is found again in *Almost by Chance a Woman: Elizabeth*. Queen Elizabeth (originally played by Rame) attempts to increase the size of her breasts. Using bee and wasp stings, provided by a nutty beautician-sorceress (originally played by Fo), she succeeds in swelling only one breast and one buttock. And in the process, she wets herself, for the second time (1997:241-46).

More recently in his book on environmental issues and global warming, *L'Apocalisse rimandata* (The apocalypse postponed), Fo is invited to a television talk show, hosted by center-right politician and occasional talk-show host, Giuliano Ferrara. The other guest is the prominent atmospheric physicist, Franco Prodi (brother of a former prime minister). Both men are outspoken skeptics of global warming and its detrimental effects. Since their last show, Ferrara and Prodi have been swelling up, becoming enormously fat. Upon seeing them, Fo exclaims, "This is terrible! But please excuse me, could this be a result of the spurious nonsense the two of you have been spewing?" (2008:11). The two inflated men are trapped inside the television studio, too large to fit through the doors. Fo tries to get help, but everyone is leaving in a panic, with the approach of a tsunami—a direct result of global warming, of course. The tsunami hits and as Fo comes to the surface, he sees the two laughing gleefully as they easily float on the water. But then like pricked aerostatic balloons they deflate and pop, and Fo wakes up from his "terrible nightmare" (2008:12). In the discussion of the carnival and the carnivalesque below, it will become clear that lampooning authority is only one function of the grotesque in Fo's theatre.

The Farce Is in Reality

There is a paradoxical element to the Fo phenomenon. Despite the fact that many of his plays are "throw-away," written quickly in order to capture current events, and the fact that they are idiomatically written for Fo and Rame to perform, they still manage to translate cross-culturally and are performed throughout the world. (See Farrell 2000a:197-211.) Part of the answer to this paradox is provided by analyzing Fo's indexical frame. One explanation as to why Fo's plays become popular across language and cultural barriers and continue to be pertinent over time is because they often touch on universal truths. In the prologue to *Anomaly*, Fo explains that his attempts to write "a grotesque satire as quickly as possible were not easy" (2004a:5). Fifteen days after the final draft was ready, they realized that it no longer worked. "Why? Because those in power had copied from us all the paradoxical material we had invented. Everything absurd was becoming real. They were copying us without even paying royalties" (6). He goes on to recount how they set out to write something so completely wild and bizarre that it could not, in any way, resemble reality. *"I'd like to see them catch up with us now.* A month later and they're on our heels!" (6, emphasis added).

Early in the play, as the Director is explaining the plot of his film to Anastasia, Fo breaks character for a metatheatric comment.

Anastasia: It's a crazy story!

Director: And grotesque!

Anastasia: Yes, grotesque, even a bit cruel, excessive! But really, two premiers with shattered craniums, exchanged pieces of brains as it they were doughnuts!

Dario: At least they won't be able to steal this scene from us! (*Audience applauds*) (2004b)

This metatheatric break alludes back to the prologue, which in turn is supported by one of the most important and prevalent themes in his thematic frame. To cite a few examples, the same idea is stated in the introduction to *Can't Pay! Won't Pay!*: "Writing this comedy we wanted to play with fantasy to the extreme. We forecast things that at the time (more than three months ago) seemed like political fiction. But then reality not only copied us but surpassed us quite a bit" (1974a:np). With regard to the joke about paying royalties, the same idea is expressed in the introduction to *The Pope and the Witch*. Fo insinuates that the pope reacted to the criticism in the play and began to express compassion for drug addicts: "At first I was upset and even thought of sending a letter to the Writers Guild: 'The pope has plagiarized me'!" (1992b:i).

This is a central theme that Fo has repeated often and that helps define the modus operandi of his theatre. The farcical elements of a given play function like a mirror that reflects the absurdities of the issues at hand. Fo has constantly made the point that the *true farce* is not in the play, but rather in the lies, deceptions, and abuses by those in power. If the absurdity of the plots and stories is an attempt to reflect the absurdity of how power is abused (lies are told, people are exploited, etc.), the farce is not actually in the play, but in the reality it is satirizing. A similar point was made by American talk-show host and journalist, Bill Moyers, who said essentially the same thing about the American political scene during the presidency of George W. Bush, in an essay entitled, "Who Needs Michael Moore When You Have the *Real* Show?" Moyers describes a litany of "absurd" and "outrageous" acts and statements by a number of people in power, starting with the president and continuing with representatives of various organizations. He concludes: "You think I'm kidding. But believe me, I couldn't make this stuff up if I wanted to. Unfortunately, I don't have to" (2004:10).[26]

In *Accidental Death of an Anarchist*, Fo suggests that people in power seem to gravitate towards repeated patterns of abuse followed by brazen and absurd explanations. The play focuses on the 1969 death of Giuseppe Pinelli, who died while being held illegally in police headquarters in Milan, as a suspect in a deadly string of bombings.[27] Police explained that he had jumped out of the window, but the evidence indicated that he most likely died of overzealous interrogations, and that the police tried to cover-up his death by throwing his body out the window. In the official police version, Pinelli was overcome by his own guilt and *jumped* out of the window. Judge Antonino Amati, who was involved in the first enquiry into Pinelli's death, specified that Pinelli was overtaken by suicidal anguish, which he termed a *raptus*, i.e. an overwhelming bout of emotional anxiety.

Fo's Matto infiltrates police headquarters and conducts an "investigation." He picks up on the absurdity of *raptus* explanation:

Matto: Let's start at the beginning and proceed in order: Around midnight the anarchist, overcome by a *raptus* (this is still you speaking Chief?), overcome by a *raptus* threw himself out of the window, ending his life on the pavement below. Now, what is a *raptus*? Bandieu says that a *raptus* is a crisis of overwhelming suicidal anguish that can strike a perfectly sane individual, if he is provoked by a violent anxiety or desperate anguish. Right?

Police Chief and Commissioner: Right.

Matto: So then, let's see what provoked this anxiety. We shall reconstruct the events, starting with your entrance.

Police Chief: Me?

Matto: Yes. Do you mind reenacting your notorious entrance?

Police Chief: Pardon. What notorious . . . ?

Matto: The one that brought on this *raptus*. (1988:24)

In 1979, while *Anarchist* was playing in London, police charged a peaceful demonstration. A school teacher, Clement Blair Peach, was struck in the head and died later in a hospital. In a TV documentary on Dario Fo, Gavin Richards, who was playing il Matto at the time, explained how the play took on new meaning: "Then the Blair Peach incident happened . . . the play was . . . really smacking home suddenly . . . and more and more the comedy was bordering on the edge of frightening" (Marks 1984). In 1980, an inquest jury into Peach's death returned the verdict: death by "misadventure."

In the United States and in Canada, controversy continues over "excited delirium." This is a term that is often used to explain why some people suddenly die while in police custody, often after being shocked with stun guns. Incoherence, agitation, and violent behavior are among the symptoms that are associated with the syndrome. It is not within the scope of this study to argue the merits of excited delirium. Suffice it to say that if in fact it is eventually proven to be groundless, it would be disturbingly akin to *raptus*.[28]

Fo endeavors to create his own brand of epic theatre that goes beyond entertainment and that delivers eye-opening messages about the abuse of power and the complacency of people living in democracies. Underlying all of this is a point well-taken: The abuse of power that goes on around us, when viewed with an ironic eye, is inherently more farcical than a staged farce. Thus under the surface of a play like *Anarchist* lies a very disturbing truth. The register of laughter that Dario Fo aims to generate is not meant to "relieve" the audience and allow them to leave the theatre refreshed and renewed. Rather it is an ironic laughter that intends to make one think and become angry. "His jeering at painful events allows the underlying tragedy to remain in the mind, but the laughter is not the nihilistic variety which suggests that all life is senseless and all systems equal, but an uncomfortable laughter followed by anger, and hence, in Fo's view, by action and hope" (Farrell 2001:100-01).

One of the problems with staging Fo's satirical farces abroad is the tendency to slip into silly clowning, losing sight of the darkness inherent in the farce. For example, in staging *Anarchist* abroad, the police are often represented, not as Fo's original, in which they were stupid and evil, but simply as stupid, and they tend to come off more as clowns or Keystone Cops. With reference to the 1980 production of *Anarchist* in London (mentioned above), Fo defined the "excessive buffoonery" as "'anti-style' . . . 'style' in the sense of a satirical form of theatre that seeks to wound, to disturb people, to hit them where it hurts" (1983:67-68). As far as Fo is concerned, if the underlying tragedy is lost, the play ends up being "a sort of surreal *pochade* where the audience cuts loose with laughter, only to leave the theatre unburdened by any indignation or disturbing thought" (1990:149-50). Although no one would suggest that Fo always gets it right, he must be given credit for his dogged endeavors to wake people up to the abuse of power around them. Perhaps Goffman is correct when he writes: "I can only suggest that he who would combat false consciousness and awaken people to their true interests has much to do, because the sleep is very deep" (1986:14).

Notes

1. "A Theory of Play and Fantasy" was originally published as an article in 1955.

2. Cf. Abrahams' study of Afro-Caribbean culture, where participation is expected of audience members (1984).

3. See Hymes 1971 and 1975. Cf. Fo's statement on narration as performance in the preceding chapter.

4. Great homage was paid to Bauman's work when the *Journal of American Folklore* dedicated a special issue to reassess its influence, over twenty years after its publication (Berger and Del Negro 2002).

5. On this point Bauman (1984:23-24) draws primarily from Gary Gossens's studies on the Chamula's traditions of verbal behavior.

6. Foley uses the term "performance arena" to refer to the interpretive frame (1995:8).

7. For a discussion of Fo's flexible frame in *Johan Padan*, see Scuderi 1998:28-32.
8. For Fo's use of ancient and medieval theatre, see Scuderi 2000a. For Fo's thoughts on epic theatre and breaking the fourth wall in popular performance, see Binni 1975:149-55.
9. An example of the latter is the play *Free Mario! Mario Is Innocent!*
10. One of Fo and Rame's most famous acts of defiance was the taking over of the Palazzina Liberty building in Milan. See Behan 2000.
11. First quoted in *Playboy* (Italian edition), December 1974. See Binni 1975:385 and Cowan 1975.
12. Dario Fo is credited with writing the text, designing the set and costumes, and directing. The music is by Fiorenzo Carpi, a long-time collaborator.
13. For *L'Anomalo bicefalo* both the text (2004a) and a videocassette (2004b), a composite of two live performances, were consulted.
14. The obstacles that as yet were not overcome are the lawsuits filed against Fo and Rame, in particular those filed by Senator Dell'Utri for defamation. On the videocassette by Planet and Atlantide, the facts about the Dell'Utri lawsuit are explained in a written introduction.
15. In 2003 it came to light that the Italian dairy corporation, Parmalat, one of the biggest companies in Europe, was embroiled in an accounting scandal, overstating its assets by anywhere from 10 to 16 billion euros.
16. My thanks to linguist Tom Cravens for his help in formulating this definition. Elsewhere in this study, *register* is used in a broader connotation, suggesting a distinctive range on a gamut of possible modes of intellectual and emotional expression.
17. Léon Chancerel (1886-1965) uses "grammelot" (1946:47) in a book that was published before Fo became a professional performer. It lends credence to Fo's assertion that the term originated with the commedia-derived French theatre. The technique however goes back at least to the proto-commedia *buffoni* (see Scuderi 2000a:54-58).
18. In Italian slang, *culo* (ass) means incredible luck.
19. The clown originated in the commedia dell'arte-derived pantomime before being adapted by circus performers. It continued as a form of comic artistry in Europe throughout the 1800s until about the 1930s. See Scuderi 1998:91-93.
20. For more on Fo and the *sotie*, see Scuderi 2000a:42-50.
21. A similar opposition is found in Fo's sketch "The Wedding at Cana" in *Mistero buffo*. See Scuderi 1998:85-86.
22. See Fo 1997:100, 275-76 and Binni 1975:150-51. In *Almost by Chance a Woman: Elizabeth* (*Quasi per caso una donna: Elisabetta*) we read in the stage directions, "At this point a technical mistake is simulated" (Fo 1997:263). A simulated accident can also be found in *The Devil in Drag* (*IlDiavolo con le zinne*) (Fo 1998:117).

23. The other is when Fo demonstrates how he creates the illusion of the dwarf to the audience.

24. This statement (quoted here from Mitchell 1999:140) was originally published in the magazine *Panorama* (June 1975) and aimed at the Italian Christian Democratic party.

25. At the time Fo looked to Communist China as an example of a functioning Marxist state (see Farrell 2001:158-64), thus allegorically the Chinese suppository releases the gasses of Fascism from within Fanfani.

26. He read this on NOW with Bill Moyers (Public Television) and published it in the *Christian Science Monitor* (Moyers 2004).

27. Inquiries conducted in the 1990s have pretty much established that the bombings were the work of neo-fascists, aided by elements of the police. For more on the background to *Anarchist*, see Mitchell 1999:101-115; Behan 2000:63-83; Farrell 2001:98-104.

28. At this point there are articles and studies, many online, linked to excited delirium, dating back to the 1990s.

Chapter Three

Ennobling Folk Culture and Re-Presenting History

Fo developed his unique approach to theatre by borrowing extensively from folk and popular traditions. Key elements that define epic-theatre are inherent to many forms of popular performance, where players do not get into character (in the Stanislavskian sense) and there is an absence of the fourth wall. These characteristics of popular performance tend to put greater emphasis on the narrative rather than on the characters. In an interview he discussed his approach to acting and explained how, by remaining out of character and detached from the play, he "tells about" the person he is playing, rather than trying to portray or become that person. In this way, the actor's primary role is that of storyteller. "This is precisely the great difference between epic theatre and art theatre" (Fo 1993). Although this takes place to some extent in all of Fo's performances, it is presented in its purest form in his *giullarata*, which is primarily an oral-derived, storytelling event. The *giullarata* shares many aspects with storytelling traditions around the world, in particular those in which a single performer both narrates the tale and acts out all of the parts.

Much of the reasoning behind Fo's penchant for folk traditions and popular theatre can be explained by his interpretation of the writings of Antonio Gramsci (1891-1937). Often developed with the Italian context specifically in mind, Gramsci's Marxist theories had a tremendous influence on Italian leftist intellectuals of Fo's generation. At the basis of Gramsci's social philosophy is the concept of *superstructure* as the cultural form of a society, which is a manifestation of the tensions inherent in the economic conflicts at its basis, that is, the *substructure*. His renowned theory of hegemony was an attempt to explain how the ruling classes keep the working classes in a subservient position by convincing them of their cultural inferiority.

For Gramsci, both language and folk culture could be studied as conceptions of the world and of life (1985:167). His theories become more relevant when one considers them in their historical context. During Gramsci's lifetime and Fo's youth, the contrast between culture of the elite classes and the popular culture of the masses in Italy was very marked. One of the most significant and obvious dividing markers was language. Italy was at the time *diglossic*. Most people spoke a dialect, i.e. a local language, at home and in their communities, while standard Italian was learned in school and used for official business, scholarship, and forms of high-culture art such as theatre and opera.[1] This linguistic situation tended to distinguish and divide the upper, more educated classes from the masses. Addressing this diglossic context, Gramsci draws a parallel between standard Italian and the literary Latin of the Middle Ages, in the sense that both were languages of a learned elite: "Italian is once again a written language and not a spoken one, a language of the erudite and not of the nation" (Q 3, par. 76).[2]

Thus while Fo's satirical farces are in Italian, his *giullarate* are performed in dialect (mainly his native Lombard with elements of Venetan and other neighboring dialects), which he considers more genuine and expressive than the standard language.[3] Of course, these performances, unlike his "throw-away" plays, require more preparation and more effort in order to communicate to audiences outside of his native region, who do not readily understand his dialect. And even when performing in his region, there is the added problem that in Italy today the dialects are fading fast. Younger generations tend to have less and less contact with and competence in their dialects. In his satirical farces, Fo sometimes has a particular character speak in dialect in order to underscore his/her popular origins, such as Donnazza in *Almost by Chance a Woman: Elizabeth* and Pizzocca in *The Devil in Drag*. In the book *L'Apocalisse rimandata*, Fo's apocalyptic vision of a future environmental crisis, many residents of industrialized Milan must abandon the city and move to the countryside, where they discover the locals are more self-sufficient in terms of food and energy. One of these rual folk, an expert on solar energy, warns the newcomers that "the common language is the dialect of the area" (2008:93).

Key to understanding where Fo sees himself in the greater Marxist-Gramscian schema is Gramsci's discussion of the different categories of intellectuals. Gramsci's basic premise is that all people are potential intellectuals, by way of possessing and using intellect. "All men are intellectuals, one could say, but not all men have the function of intellectuals in society" (Q 12, par. 1). Applying the conventional denotation of the term, he identifies *traditional intellectuals* by their profession. For example, in the upper classes these would include scholars, philosophers, scientists, literati, etc., who, according to Gramsci, are wont to consider themselves elite. There are also *organic intellectuals* who develop "organically" from within a given social class. These intellectuals are not defined by their profession as much as by their function as thinkers and organizers within their class. His worldview had a privileged place for the organic intellectual of the working class as an engine for creating a new social order.

To understand the masses, it is important for the Marxist intellectual, whether traditional or organic, to study their culture. Gramsci discusses the problem of conventional scholarship, which, in his opinion, typically considered folk culture as outlandish and quaint. He argues for the importance of formulating a serious approach to the study and teaching of folklore, in order to give the masses a better understanding of their own culture. It is the task of the Marxist intellectual to give to the masses a sense of dignity for their culture.

> Folklore should not be conceived as something bizarre, strange, or picturesque, but as something serious which should be taken seriously. This is the only way to assure that the teaching of folklore will be more efficient and will truly determine the birth of a new culture among the popular masses, that is, the barrier between modern culture and popular culture or folklore will disappear. (Q 27, par. 1)

Validating and ennobling folk culture has always been a great part of Fo's mission and informs the overall raison d'être of his theatre. In fact, he views the function of theatre itself as an instrument for bringing culture back to the people. As early as 1971 he stated "it is the duty of every intellectual to reconstruct folk culture, which has been stolen and falsified, in order to give it back to the people and make of it the highest and most progressive instrument of the revolution. And this work must be repeated with the masses, without end" (1992a:76-77). In the opening of his play *The Worker Knows 300 words, the Boss Knows 1,000—That's Why He's the Boss* (*L'operaio conosce 300 parole il padrone 1000 per questo lui è il padrone*), several members of the Communist party are removing books from the library of their *casa del popolo* (party-run community center), while discussing how most members of the working class do not read anymore. As they become curious and read passages from the various books they are handling, visions of their Marxist forefathers and other characters appear and interact. At one point the specter of Antonio Gramsci succinctly expresses the crux of Fo's interpretation of Gramscian ideas on folk culture and the role of the Marxist intellectual with relation to the folk:

> We must stop thinking of the working class as marionettes, who don't know, who can't know, because they don't have culture. The working class knows because they are at the vanguard of the people, because the people have a great culture. Bourgeois power, aristocratic power, and the Church have in great part destroyed it, buried it. But it is our duty to help them retrieve it. (1975:107)

Fo's collaboration with Nuovo Canzoniere Italiano (New Italian songbook) was a turning point with regard to his understanding of folk culture and oral traditions. Formed in 1962, the NCI focused on researching popular culture, popular history, and protest movements as expressed in traditional songs. Based on their research they produced informative literature, sound recordings, and stage shows. Working with NCI, Fo gained a greater understanding of the oral tradition and a familiarity with the concepts of folklore research methodology. He and Rame collaborated with NCI to produce the stage show *Ci ragiono e canto* (I think it over and sing) in 1966, which featured popular performers from various regions of Italy, singing traditional songs with theatrical choreography. However, Fo had various disagreements with the members of NCI, which eventually resulted in the end of their collaboration.[4] In discussing some of the bases for these disagreements, Farrell explains, "some NCI members were outraged when Dario wrote some musical numbers of his own which he wanted to pass off as original pieces" (2001:69). However, there is an interesting passage in Gramsci's writing that might help to explain his justification for this:

> A division or distinction of popular songs, formulated by Ermolao Rubieri: 1) songs composed by the people and for the people; 2) those composed for the people but not by the people; 3) those written neither by the people nor for the people, but adapted by the people because they conform to their manner of thinking and feeling. It seems to me that all popular songs can and must be reduced to this third category, since that which distinguishes a popular song, in the context of a nation and its culture, is neither the artistic factor nor its historic origin, but the way in which it conceives the world and life, in contrast to official society. (Q 5, par. 156)

Gramsci goes on to explain that the folk cannot be reduced simplistically to a homogeneous cultural collectivity. The various combinations of cultural elements that come together from various strata of society make this impossible. In keeping with his role as an organic, Marxist intellectual, Fo believed he was justified in writing songs for the folk, as long as the themes were compatible with their thinking, feeling, and worldview, in contrast to hegemonic culture.

Pranks and the Re-Presentation of History

Fo puts great emphasis on history and on more than one occasion has stated this axiom *he attributes* to Gramsci: "It is difficult to know where you want to go, without knowing whence you came" (Fo 1987:109; 1990:140). The function of history in his theatre is complex, paradoxical, if not contradictory. He is interested in history, has studied it, refers to it often, and has various plays contextualized in the past.[5] However, he takes great liberties in re-presenting history subjectively, often presenting his own inventions as facts or as historically accurate. "Fo was never moved by any undue reverence for the historical authenticity of material when he believed its immediate theatrical impact could be enhanced by rewriting" (Farrell 2001:70). This aspect of Fo has been well documented and there is no need to retrace it here in detail. It will suffice to simply highlight a few things to make the point.

Fo's masterpiece, *Mistero buffo*, first produced in 1969, was the work that brought to light his penchant for mixing fact with fiction. It eventually became clear that there were no historical texts, as Fo had claimed, for certain sketches, such as "Birth of the *Giullare*" and "Boniface VIII." Furthermore his inventions went beyond stories and texts:

> On the first outing, Dario illustrated the performance with slides of medieval frescos and paintings, but discovered himself short of some images. No problem for a man of his talents. He spent the next day executing the images in the required style, photographed them himself and used the slides the following night as a reproduction of the work of an unknown master from the Dark Ages. (Farrell 2001:89)

Michele Straniero, a former member of NCI, challenges the authenticity of Fo's assertions concerning *Mistero buffo* and the Middle Ages in a book entitled *Giullari e Fo*. In it he accused Fo of distorting historical reality. "Dario Fo frequently deforms history, not only in his theatrical performances, where it would be legitimate, at least as far as it has to do with artistic imagination and not with unilateral propaganda, but even in other instances in which historical truth should be respected . . ." (1978:142). This book was instrumental in bringing many of these discrepancies to the attention of other scholars and is often cited in this context.

With the debate made public, Fo was obliged to address this aspect of his theatre. In his *Manuale minimo dell'attore* (*The Tricks of the Trade*) he addresses the issue, perhaps somewhat overstating his defense, while simultaneously adding a touch of mystique: "Well yes, it's true, I often make things up. But beware and let it be clear. The stories that I fabricate will seem terribly authentic, almost obvious, while the improbable and paradoxical ones, the ones you'd swear were invented, are all authentic and documentable. I am a professional liar" (1987:4). But shortly following this proclamation, we read, "I've always said that the supercritical, nitpicking pedants are those who, when you show them the moon, they look at your finger, and in particular the nail, in order to guess how long ago you cut it" (1987:4). This could be taken as an attempt to distinguish himself and his mission from the conventional, fact-gathering work of traditional, upper-class intellectuals. Fo, the organic intellectual of the working class, tries to move society forward. Using his theatre as an instrument of communication, he endeavors to enlighten the masses to the importance of their culture, to their political situation, and their historical victimization by the ruling classes. By contrast, the traditional pedant is overly concerned with minutia, which often serves only to hinder the process. This being said, there are other aspects to Fo's historical inventions and the way they function in his theatre that warrant consideration.

The *giullarata Johan Padan Discovers America*, first produced in 1991, tells the tale of an Italian rogue who escapes the Inquisition in Europe and stows away on one of Columbus' ships during his fourth voyage to the New World. In the prologue of a filmed performance, Fo explains that, in preparation for the play, he read various accounts by European explorers and adventurers to the New World, such as Hans Staden, Diego Nalgiar, and Cabeza de Vaca. He states emphatically that the account which impressed him the most and that he used the most was by Michele Da Cuneo, "who comes clean on the stuff that Columbus tries to gloss over or sugarcoat" (1992c). Similarly in Fo's prologue to the English translation of the play, he distinguishes Da Cuneo's account as the most important from among the ones he consulted, emphasizing its objective realism (Fo 2001:xii). However, the circumstances behind the discovery of Da Cuneo's letter points to the distinct possibility that Fo has encoded a clue to understanding his manipulation of history.

Da Cuneo, a native of Savona in Liguria, was a friend of the Columbus family. He sailed with Columbus on his second voyage in 1493, serving as the admiral's man-at-arms. In 1885 Olindo Guerrini, poet and director of the library at the University of Bologna, announced that he had discovered a copy of a lengthy letter by Da Cuneo, which recounted his adventures in the New World. The letter, dated October 1495, is addressed to one Gerolamo Annari, a fellow Savonese. Initially there were some questions about possible anachronisms in the writing style, indicating possible forgery. But the letter was officially checked for authenticity and was ultimately included as part of the official documents, collected for the 1892 quadricentennial celebration of Columbus' first voyage. But in 1942 a certain Virgilio Brocchi published a book entitled *Le beffe di Olindo*, which translates as "Olindo's pranks." As it turns out, Guerrini was a notorious prankster, whose practical jokes included passing off his own works under the names of nonexistent authors. Brocchi suggests that the Da Cuneo letter could be yet another of Guerrini's scholarly hoaxes.

In an article that addresses the possible apocryphal nature of the letter, Ignazio Bignardelli argues that for various reasons it is unlikely that Guerrini either wrote or altered the Da Cuneo letter. Unlike his other lighthearted scholarly hoaxes, he explains, this one had possible serious consequences for the field of history and geographic exploration, and threatened to mar the reputation of all Bolognese scholarship (1962:178,181). He notes discrepancies such as the date of the letter: Columbus' returned from the expedition in June 1496, yet the letter is dated October 1495. He points out that in February 1494 and 1495, Columbus sent groups of men back to Spain. Da Cuneo may have sailed back in 1495, making the date of his letter perfectly plausible. However, when all is said and done, Bignardelli concedes that he cannot provide definitive proof, which must wait for either more sophisticated means of testing or for the discovery of the original copy. And he acknowledges the situation Guerrini created for himself, for "being born a joker and having that notorious reputation is often a serious problem, because one runs the very probable risk of creating doubts, completely unjustified, concerning the validity of one's assertions, no matter how veracious and serious" (1962:177).

It is precisely this principle which applies to Fo and the state of his "authentic and documentable" facts. At a certain point, it became useless to try and verify his historical assertions. His appeal to the authority of history became a part of his performance, and like many forms of entertainment, requires a suspension of disbelief on the part of the audience. Other functions will be taken up shortly. As for the possible clue, he may have purposely encoded it or it may just be one big coincidence. In the spirit of the prankster, what better way of creating a ruse than to cite the authority of a spurious historical document? Certainly asking Fo directly would serve no purpose! However, there are several tantalizing connections between Fo and Guerrini that are more than coincidental. The first being that Guerrini's discovery was not too long before the quadricentennial celebration, and his document succeeded in being included among the officially recognized memorabilia. Similarly, Fo's *Johan Padan* was timed to coincide with the 1992 quincentennial celebrations, one hundred years later.

If Guerrini was indeed a notorious prankster, so was Fo, even before beginning his theatrical career. As a university student, among his prank-loving college pals, Dario was known as "the Puckish mischief-maker-in-chief." In one instance he and his friends climbed up the scaffolding bridge between two buildings at the Brera Art Academy in Milan where Fo was studying. Using rope, they managed to haul up all of the parked bicycles, "leaving them dangling in an elaborate pattern across the façade of the *Accademia*."

> The group's most celebrated escapade involved spreading the word that Pablo Picasso himself was about to visit Milan. They persuaded friendly journalists to carry the story in their papers and tickets were sold for a reception to welcome the great artist to Milan. A janitor from the Brera, who apparently had some resemblance to Picasso, was put on the Paris express a couple of stations up the line and was met at Milan's central station by a crowd, including both false and genuine photographers. (Farrell 2001:19-20)

Another quality that would naturally render Guerrini close to Fo's heart was the fact that he was a confirmed "mangiapreti" (Bignardelli 1962:180). This colorful Italian term translates literally as "priest-eater" and denotes someone who is rabidly anticlerical. Fo's objection to the Catholic Church as a manipulative institution of power and corruption is well documented and plays a part in his thematic code, running through many of his works, in particular the sketch "Boniface VIII" from *Mistero buffo* and *The Pope and the Witch*.[6]

Various Functions of History in Fo's Theatre

There is the possibility that Fo foresaw that someday he would be challenged on his historical facts and calculated a priori what role this would then play in his theatre. But more than likely, the way in which he uses history developed over time, as his theatre matured into an organic, interrelated system of theatrical techniques and mechanisms, supporting political themes and messages. In either case, when contextualized in terms of carnival culture, it should become clear that at one level Fo's bogus appeal to historical *auctoritas* is a prank—albeit a prank that makes a point—and fits into his greater carnival frame. At the same time, Fo's re-presentation of history has become an essential part of his theatre and provides him with a great deal of flexibility. He can refer to a historical past, which he molds like clay to fit his sense of purpose, in the same way he fashioned slides of "medieval art" to support his discourse on *Mistero buffo*. With the readiness of historical flexibility, Fo uses history and historical settings in various ways.

If Fo's idea of a flexible historical past most likely evolved over time, the technique of *reversal* or *inversion* was certainly with Fo from the beginning of his performance career. His first significant engagement as a professional performer in the early 1950s was *Poer nano* (Poor dwarf), a radio show that consisted of songs and stories. He retold well-known tales, including Bible stories, Shakespearean plays, and historical events, applying a technique he learned from his earliest experiences in verbal art. From the local storytellers of his childhood, the *fabulatori*, Fo learned many "narrative strategies" and "techniques of storytelling" (1990:23-24). One such technique, the reversal, consists of retelling a well-known story with zany and ironic twists, often making the traditional hero look anything but heroic and presenting the villain as victim. In the stories of *Poer nano*, God is absentminded; Cain is a pathetic simpleton, living in the shadow of his golden-boy brother; Othello is not a Moor, but an albino, and so on. Underlying these zany reversals is a subversion of many of the conventions of official culture, in particular the tendency to present morality in simplistic, black-and-white terms.[7] Fo explains:

> The key point of these stories was always paradox, opposites and contraries . . . These reversals were not done just for their own sake, but were an absolute refusal to accept the logic of convention, a rebellion against the moral contingent which always sees good on one side and evil on the other . . . The comedy and the liberating entertainment lies in the discovery that the contrary stands up better than the commonplace . . . There is also the fun of desecrating and demolishing the sacred and untouchable monuments of religious tradition. (Mitchell 1999:53-54)

This was of course more relevant in its historical context, and as a result, ahead of its time. Since the 1950s, there have been many challenges to conventional ways of presenting morality, and we tend to view heroes and villains of history in a more complex and sophisticated ways. The technique of reversal was carried over and remained with Fo throughout his career. It ties into his concept of dialectic, which means "that something can be viewed in five different ways. . . . Truth has a thousand faces, not just one" (1993).

Fo's favorite historical period begins in the later Middle Ages and continues through the Renaissance, spanning roughly the eleventh to the sixteenth centuries. *Storia vera di Piero d'Angera che alla crociata non c'era* (True story of Piero d'Angera who was not at the Crusade) takes place at the time of the first Crusade. Although to date this play was never performed, it was written around 1960 and may be his first full-length play in a historical setting. What follows is a list of list of his major plays that are set in the medieval/Renaissance period, in the order in which they were first performed. *Isabella, Three Sailing Ships and a Con Man* is a play within a play. The frame story is set in the sixteenth century, and the performance within the play is set about 30 years earlier, during the time of Columbus' expeditions. This was Fo's first full-length historical work that was performed. *Always Blame the Devil* takes place at the end of the thirteenth century. Fo's first *giullarata*, *Mistero buffo*, is in the tradition of medieval street performance and an attempt to recreate certain aspects of medieval culture. It was revised various times, and *Obscene Fables*, which consists of several sketches in the medieval period, may be considered another edition of *Mistero buffo*. *Almost by Chance a Woman: Elizabeth* is about the famous monarch of the English Renaissance.

Hellequin, Harlekin, Arlecchino is a series of sketches based on the most famous stock character of the commedia dell'arte. *Johan Padan*, once again, is set during Columbus' expeditions. *The Devil in Drag* takes place at the end of the sixteenth century. Fo pays homage to the sixteenth-century Venetan playwright in two related works: *Dario Fo incontra* [meets] *Ruzzante* (with other actors) and *Dario Fo recita* [performs] *Ruzzante* (a solo). *The Holy Jester Francis* is about Saint Francis of Assisi, who lived from 1182 to 1226. Many more examples of Fo's interest in this period may be given. A few of the most recent ones to date come from his book *Apocalisse*. As the people of Milan hold public fora to discuss how they are going to restructure under the new conditions (which include the end of fossil fuels), they draw lessons from the "Lombard republics of the Middle Ages," and from "the statutes of the city-state of Gubbio, at the end of the twelfth century" (2008:110, 112).

There are certain advantages in setting a play in another time and place. For example, the comedies of the Roman playwright Plautus were in the style of the *palliata*, "in Greek dress." While Plautus' *palliatae* were always set in the Greek world, the satire obviously targeted Roman society. Erich Segal discusses the various motives and advantages of this technique, which would not have been possible in the *togata* plays, "in Roman dress" (1968:31-41). For the ancient Romans, the Greeks were considered anti-Roman, lacking virtue and prone to overindulgence. Mocking Greeks allowed Plautus to heap on the satire. "Plautus, of course, is deliberately excusing himself for comic effect." Segal offers an analogous example in Pierre Beaumarchais' play, *The Barber of Seville*. In a metatheatrical moment, Bartholo ironically reminds Rosine, "nous ne sommes pas ici en France" (1968:33).

Similarly, Fo's use of time parallels Plautus' use of space. Like Plautus' "Greeks," Fo's audiences can more readily accept a higher degree of cruelty, barbarism, and blatant abuse of power back in former times. One way the connection can be reinforced is by means of his indexical frame, which runs across his performances. With the famous sketch of "Boniface VIII," in *Mistero buffo*, Fo painted a grim picture of debauchery and abuse of power by the corrupt medieval pope, for whom Dante had reserved a place in hell (Canto 19). Later when Fo targeted a contemporary pope, John

Paul II in *The Pope and the Witch*, the satire's force was strengthened by his earlier criticism of ecclesiastical abuses of power. Whereas Boniface openly had concubines and could simply order the torture and/or execution of an enemy, in a contemporary context, the crimes of Fo's John Paul II are once removed and provide deniability, much like certain alleged activities of Swiss Banks.[8] The underlying message is that Catholic popes have a long tradition of abusing power. Although the Catholic Church does not wield the same level of power it did in the past, the tendency to abuse it is still there.

Even when Fo's historical plays satirize human behavior in a given period, which on one level can be taken at face value, they often allude to more recent people and events. *The Devil in Drag*, set in northern Italy during the sixteenth century, amply illustrates this. The protagonist, good Judge Alfonso de Tristano, shares similarities with Antonio Di Pietro, the leading magistrate in the Italian "clean hands" campaign, which sought to root out corruption in Italian politics (Farrell 2001:266). De Tristano's maid Pizzocca speaks directly to the audience to explain the fate of honest judges: "In this city intelligent, courageous, and honest judges have a hard life. When they are about to uncover the misdeeds of delinquents and murderers, low-flying crows appear, spreading gossip and slander, and then they blow them up! They kill them!" (1998:13). Later in another direct address, she praises her master's judicial acumen, proclaiming "this judge is a great hawk!" (27). In Italian "hawk" is *falco,* and this may well be a reference to the slain antimafia judge, Giovanni Falcone, who was successfully investigating and prosecuting top mafia bosses in his native Sicily. On May 23, 1992, while driving on a highway, Falcone, his wife, and three agents were killed by an enormous bomb. Although *The Devil in Drag* takes place in a faraway time, the plight of the honest man who challenges corruption has not changed. The character of Judge De Tristano is an obvious allegory of present-day, honest judges.

Fo's plays set in the present, such as *Accidental Death, Can't Pay, Won't Pay,* and *Anomaly,* are often designed to target immediate social and political issues. On the other hand, by creating a dialogue between past and present, the historical plays can expand the range of the satire and allow for multifaceted levels of meaning.

This leaves the satire more open to interpretation and thus may be aimed at more than one target simultaneously. A well-noted example is *Isabella, Three Sailing Ships and a Con Man*. In a Chinese-box structure, similar to but not as complex as *Anomaly*, Fo plays an actor who plays Columbus. The actor has been condemned for performing a play by Rojas, who was in trouble with the Inquisition. This alludes personally to Fo and Rame's ill-fated venture in television in 1962 (the year before *Isabella*), with their program *Canzonissima*. Their sketches were constantly being censored and cut, which ultimately led to their walking out. Columbus' dealings with the powerful Spanish court allude to Fo's attempts to deal with the power structure of Italian state-run television. The message is also expanded to include all intellectuals who compromise themselves by trying to deal with conventional power players. As Fo himself said, "the play was a criticism of the 1963 'historic compromise,' in which the Socialist Party joined forces with the Christian Democrats to form a centre-left government, and the Communist Party began to consider joining the alliance" (Mitchell 1999:75). With a metatheatrical "misunderstanding," the satire leveled at the Spanish court of Ferdinand and Isabella is redirected at the Spanish government, which at the time was under the dictatorship of Franco. Joan the Madwoman immediately catches her anachronism: "In fact, it can't be that Franco. We're in the first part of the sixteenth century" (1966:78).[9]

The device of reversal, which Fo applies constantly to historical figures, is a defining quality of his historical plays. It serves to challenge the status of icons, question conventional notions of history, and avoid simplistic and cathartic resolutions.

> Fo offers contradictory codes and values that generate disresolution. . . . Fo's investigative-expansive mode of dramaturgy does not seek a cohesive conclusion or holistic, unified meaning, but rather a dynamic, fluctuating collection of variables that reveal the variability and permeability of dichotomous socio-cultural demarcations. (Reynolds and Segal 2003:248)

In *Isabella, Three Sailing Ships and a Con Man*, Fo applies iconoclastic reversal primarily to the characters of Columbus and Queen Isabella. Columbus, an accomplished navigator with innovative ideas, is also the con man of the title, who uses deception and underhanded means to attain his ends. He is neither the history-book hero nor a villain. His character is more human, presented with strengths, weaknesses, self-interest, and pathos. In his final speech, he bemoans the plight of the person who tries to play power games with the powerful. Thus he simultaneously alludes to three things: Fo's experience with Italian television; the intellectual who tries to compromise with the power structure; and the "historic compromise."

> The story has ended. Here I am, reduced to a schmo. . . . But the fault is all mine. I had started out so well. But then between the underhandedness of others and my wanting to be shrewd—yes, even I was shrewd, in a world of cunning and shrewdness—I managed to stake out my little throne among the thrones of my superiors. Ah, those superiors, who, as soon as they needed to step on my little throne, *crack*, they sent me rolling below, amongst the poor sods from whence I came. . . . (1966:85)

Queen Isabella is presented, to some extent, as open-minded and intelligent, certainly more so than King Ferdinand. She adopts certain Moorish customs, such as frequent bathing, and concedes that in many ways they are more civilized (1966:16). She entreats Ferdinand to stop the war against the Moors, because they are the only link to Egypt and Persia. Paradoxically, she then provides him with the necessary funding, as if giving in to a petulant child (14, 17-18). When Ferdinand asks her to sign a decree to expel the Jews and appropriate their wealth, Isabella refuses: "I am a queen, not the daughter of a whore" (45). In Italian the expression "son of a whore" (*figlio di puttana*) corresponds in connotation to the English "son of a bitch." But it is an ironic proclamation because shortly thereafter, when the coffers are depleted and her interests are at stake, we learn that she indeed signed the decree (47). Years later, in the introduction to the performance of the related play, *Johan Padan*, Fo simply refers to Isabella directly as a "figlia di puttana" (1992c).

In *Elizabeth*, Fo presents the aging English monarch as paranoid, indecisive, and overly concerned with her appearance and sexuality. Shakespeare is frequently alluded to but never physically appears in the play. Fo presents him as more akin to a working-class revolutionary playwright (at least as seen by Elizabeth), suggesting affiliations with himself. For the most part, Fo tends to create his Shakespeare in his own image as "a writer whose work illustrated his relationship with contemporary society." One again, the play addresses a number of issues: "Dario used the piece to discuss the birth of the modern state, to return to the theme of commitment and the intellectual and even to refer to the Moro kidnapping" (Farrell 2001:245).[10]

> By referencing and refashioning the iconography of the Renaissance, namely Elizabeth I and Shakespeare, to address twentieth-century issues, Fo creates competing spaces that move audiences backward and forward from early modern England to contemporary Italy to the critical future. These two fictionalized historical figures, the onstage tyrannical monarch and the offstage working-class hero, serve as conduits for both contemporary counter-thought and the ideology of early modern England; they generate a space-time continuum that reminds audiences of the transhistorical legacy of oppressive state apparatuses, the multivariate forms of oppression manifested by official cultures, and the ever-present presence of voices of dissent. (Reynolds and Segal 2003:249)

Fo was inspired by Gramscian social philosophy, which saw folk and popular culture as an important basis upon which to build a new Italian society. He began to form a theatre that had as one of its primary foci the validation and ennobling of folk culture. A major breakthrough was when he realized that many of the underpinnings of epic theatre were to be found in numerous popular performance traditions. He then consciously adapted techniques of these traditions as a means of reevaluating folk and popular culture. Thus, in a certain sense, the culture provided the tools to evaluate itself.

At some point and for some reason—perhaps based on his interpretation of some of Gramsci's writing—Fo justified touching up or creating aspects of folk culture, as long as it was pertinent to the folk. This approach was extended to history. Perhaps the representation of history is based (albeit loosely) on interpretations of Gramsci, and perhaps in part it was justified by the knowledge that history has always been written and presented by members of official culture. The following chapters will explore the central aspect of Fo's use of folk culture: the European carnival. This will help to explain his penchant for medieval/Renaissance settings. It will also help to explain how the re-presentation of history—whether intended a priori or not—became an integral part of his greater carnival frame.

Notes

1. Charles A. Ferguson (1959) was the first to present a systemized approach to studying diglossia. It should be underscored that in Italy, the local languages (categorized regionally as Sicilian, Lombard, etc.) as well as standard Italian all derive from spoken Latin, and are thus all related.

2. Passages from Antonio Gramsci's writing are from *Quaderni del carcere* (*Prison Notebooks*) (Gramsci 1975), and will be designated by the notebook number (Q for *quaderno*) followed by the paragraph number.

3. See Scuderi 1998:5-10; 21-25 on the *giullarata* and other storytelling traditions, and Scuderi 2000a:54-58 on the language of the *giullarata*.

4. Fo revived the show in 1969 and again in 1973, without NCI. For more on Fo's collaboration and disagreements with NCI, see Mitchell 1999:82-84 and Farrell 2001:68-71. In 1975 Fo wrote and produced *La giullarata*, a performance involving Sicilian folk singers.

5. A recent book by Fo, *Sant'Ambrogio e l'invenzione di Milano* (Saint Ambrose and the creation of Milan) (Fo 2009), is an historical work set in the declining years of the Roman Empire in the fourth century.

6. Fo's criticism is aimed at the abuses of the Catholic Church. Like Gramsci (Q 27, par. 1), he acknowledges the importance of folk religion in popular culture. See Scuderi 1998:69-77; 81-89.

7. For more on the dialogues of *Poer nano*, see Pizza 1996:123-58.

8. Fo's criticism of ecclesiastical power in the *Pope and the Witch* includes the Church's indirect dealings with the mafia, who wish to keep drugs illegal, and the Church's stance on abortion. See Scuderi 1998:38-40, 95-98.

9. Much has been written about how these issues play in *Isabella*. See Mitchell 1999:75-78; Holm 2000:127-37; Farrell 2001:64-65; and Soriani 2007:100-29.

10. In 1978 Red Brigade terrorists captured and eventually killed Aldo Moro, a leader of the Christian Democratic party. For more on Fo and the Moro case, see Farrell 2002.

Chapter Four

The European Carnival from Liminal to *Liminoid*

Fo's interest in the carnival and the imprint it has left on his plays is the most significant and comprehensive aspect of his exploration and utilization of folk culture. A discussion of the carnival must perforce be included in an analysis of the interacting frames and mechanisms of his theatre. Carnivalesque elements abound and run prevalently throughout his works. They comprise a carnival frame, a defining quality of his overall thematic or indexical frame. The carnival represents one of the most important and pervasive aspects of European folk culture. Its influence can be seen in literature, theatre, and the visual arts. Since an extensive investigation of such a huge topic is not within the scope of this study, this chapter will instead focus on those aspects that are most relevant to Fo. The intent is to momentarily set aside a direct discussion of Fo's theatre, and provide the historical and anthropological background of its carnival frame. Specifically it will concentrate on the origins of the grotesque and subversive elements that often define the carnival. The following chapters will then examine Fo's use of the carnival, in order to bring to light more detailed and nuanced functions of these grotesque and subversive principles. His carnival frame encompasses various indexical themes, creates multilayered statements and messages, and defines his approach to history and anthropology. An investigation of his use of the carnival provides a broad-spectrum view of his theatre.

Fertility Rites

In his book *The Day the Universe Changed*, science historian James Burke states that "nature is disordered, powerful and chaotic, and through fear of the chaos we impose system on it" (1995:11). Carnival was originally "a propitiatory celebration of the earth's fertility" (Toschi 1976:167), which has its roots in ancient Indo-European rites, based on solar and lunar phases. Assuring the return of the sun, the rebirth of spring, and an abundance of crops, carnivals harks back to prehistoric agricultural societies and their cosmologies. As often is the case in primary cultures, social order and cosmological order were intrinsically linked, with the belief that the human rituals had an effect, not only on themselves, but also on the workings of nature and of the cosmos.

Over the course of millennia, the people that comprised the original Indo-European stock dispersed, resettled, developed distinct cultures and languages, and interacted with other peoples. Each geographic area settled by Indo-European people presented a unique landscape with varied fauna and flora. Each area therefore presented a diverse system of symbols to the human imagination. The seasons came and went at different times with different intensities. As a result, carnival rites manifested themselves throughout the Indo-European world with great variations and were celebrated at different times of the year. Yet despite the many differences, there are unifying elements that suggest a primordial common origin for rites that were celebrated all over Europe, Persia, and northern India.

The various forms of carnival celebrations shared a number of similarities that allow us to talk about a European carnival tradition. First of all, carnival consisted of a temporary suspension of the normative world order. This period of suspension was marked by revelry and celebration, as well as a leveling of social classes, so that no one was in a position of privilege or power. A symbol was created or a person chosen to embody or personify carnival. In areas with Celtic substrata, for example, this often took the form of a giant (that shared qualities with the mythical Gargantua), an animal, most often a bear; or a wild man of the forest, often with ursine qualities (Walter 2006:4, 79). In many other geographic areas, a member of the community was chosen. Although there were a few places where the image of an animal or a giant was used, in all the regions of Italy choosing of a member of the community to personify the carnival was by far the most prevalent tradition. The person chosen was most often referred to as Carnival or the Carnival King (Toschi 1976:123-24; 134-39). The Carnival King ruled over the period of suspended world-order, hence the epithet, "Lord of Misrule." Finally, at the end of the celebration, which could vary significantly from place to place, the embodiment of carnival was ceremonially destroyed. The Effigy was decapitated or burned, and in ancient times the Carnival King was executed.[1] The carnival was over and world order was restored. With the passing of time, the execution was either enacted, or, in a few areas, the human Carnival King was eventually replaced by some sort of puppet or effigy. In some places, replacing a live person with an effigy happened just before the execution (Toschi 1976:130-31).

In its origins, carnival is a rite of passage. Although rites of passage are generally associated with an individual's passing through life stages of birth, puberty, marriage, and death, they "are not confined to culturally defined life-crises," and refer also to the process of entire communities passing from one state to another (Turner 1967:94-95). In discussing rites of passage, including "those associated with seasonal changes for an entire society," Victor Turner refers to the stages of ritual that Van Gennep designated as *separation, transition,* and *incorporation.* Based on the Latin *limen* (threshold), Van Gennep designates these three stages of temporal-spatial transition as *preliminal, liminal,* and *postliminal.*

Separation brings the participants into "a cultural realm which is defined as 'out of time,' i.e. beyond or outside the time which measures secular processes and routines. . . . In the case of members of a society, it implies collectively moving from all that is socially and culturally involved in an agricultural season" (Turner 1982:24). In the transitional or liminal stage, "the ritual subjects pass through a period and area of ambiguity, a sort of social limbo." Finally, for the participants in a collective rite of passage, incorporation represents the return to the social status quo, whereby "no change in status may be involved, but they have been ritually prepared for a whole series of changes in the nature of the cultural and ecological activities to be undertaken and of the relationships they will then have with others—all of these holding good for a specific quadrant of the annual productive-cycle" (1982:25).

The process of constructing an effigy or choosing a Carnival King to initiate the carnival period, marks the separation from the social/cosmological norms that govern life. His symbolic execution marks the end of the ritual and the community's incorporation into a restored world order. The celebrations take place during the transitional period, framed between these two points. Within this liminal phase, "a complex sequence of episodes in sacred space-time may also include subversive and ludic (or playful) events" (Turner 1982:27). During Carvinal's realm the suspension of social order allows maximum revelry. In the prehistoric period, when the ritual was of utmost importance to the survival of the community, the revelry was required by all members.

Ritual Symbols

In *The Forest of Symbols*, his study of the Ndembu people of Zambia, Turner explores the nature of rituals and the importance of their related symbols. He defines ritual as "prescribed formal behavior for occasions not given over to technological routine, having reference to beliefs in mystical beings or powers" (1967:19). To define symbol, he distinguishes it from a sign: Unlike a sign, that is an expression of a known thing, a symbol is an expression of a relatively unknown fact, which is nevertheless recognized or postulated as existing (1967:26).[2] He identifies three properties of a dominant ritual symbol: 1) *condensation*, where many things and actions are represented in a single formation; 2) *unification of disparate significata*, which allows the symbol to bracket together diverse ideas and phenomena; and 3) *polarization of meaning*. The latter brings together elements of the "ideological pole," that refers to components of moral and social order, and the "sensory pole," natural and physiological phenomena and processes (1967:28).

The effigy or person that embodies the carnival is the dominant symbol of the ritual and, as such, comprehends the properties outlined by Turner. In the Italian context, this would be Carnival or the Carnival King. Toschi expresses a sense of the symbol's quality of condensation when he states, "the people tend to transform the facts and elements of their daily experiences into myths, and such tendencies reach their apex, being concretized in personification" (1976:123). The paradoxical and oxymoronic title, "Lord of Misrule," itself gives a sense of the symbol's ability to bring together disparate *significata*. The breadth of the Carnival King's symbolic condensation becomes evident when we consider his other major function as scapegoat, which comes at the end of the ritual. The important moment comes before his execution. First Carnival publically proclaims his last testament, which includes advice, recommendations, and allusions to the conduct of his compatriots. "Joking, biting, and satirical," the testament is delivered in typical carnivalesque register. "The satire has the explicit function of public denouncement, as well as the liberation from the collective evil committed by the community's members."[3] Carnival's testament is usually followed by his funeral rites that define him as the embodiment of all that is "old, bad, and needs to be eliminated" (Toschi 1976:229). In his function as scapegoat then, he embodies both the old year as well as the community's misdeeds. Taking the ills of the community upon himself, with his execution he cleanses the society and restores its relationship to the cosmos. With the rite of passage completed, the community may begin the new annual cycle with a clean slate. Thus the Carnival King has two primary functions: 1) as Lord of Misrule during the liminal period, and 2) as scapegoat to cleanse the community and prepare it for incorporation back to quotidian life. The two functions, albeit distinct, work as part of the same propitiatory, transitional, and cleansing process.

As for the polarization of meaning, the Carnival King comprehends elements of both poles. His association with the ideological pole is evident: He is the focal point that leads the community from an old to a new social order. At the ideological pole "is found the cluster of *significata* that refer to components of the moral and social order of . . . society, to principles of social organization, to kinds of corporate groupings, and to the norms and values inherent in structural relationships" (Turner 1967:28). Concurrently, "at the sensory pole, the meaning is closely related to the outward form of the symbol." In this case, the Lord of Misrule reigns over the ludic and licentious celebrations, which are freed from the interdicts that govern sober and responsible social behavior. In opposition to the norms and values that guide and control persons as members of social groups and categories is a cluster of *significata* that appeal to "the lowest common denominator of human feeling . . . even flagrantly physiological" (Turner 1967:28). In his discussion of

Ndembu symbols, "at their sensory poles of meanings," Turner lists "blood, male and female genitalia, semen, urine, and feces" (1967:29), reminiscent of Bakhtin's "bodily lower stratum." Besides "the area of the genital organs, the fertilizing and generating stratum," Bakhtin explains, "in the images of urine and excrement is preserved the essential link with birth, fertility, renewal, welfare" (1984:148). Thus the Carnival King as,

> the basic unit of ritual, the dominant symbol, encapsulates the major properties of the total ritual process which brings about this transmutation. Within its framework of meanings, the dominant symbol brings the ethical and jural norms of society into close contact with strong emotional stimuli. In the action situation of ritual, with its social excitement and directly physiological stimuli, such as music, singing, dancing, alcohol, incense, and bizarre modes of dress, the ritual symbol, we may perhaps say, effects an interchange of qualities between its poles of meaning. Norms and values, on the one hand, become saturated with emotion, while the gross and basic emotions become ennobled through contact with social values. (Turner 1967:30)

Masks

The Carnival King was certainly the dominant and most comprehensive symbol of the rite. But there were also myriad minor or secondary symbols related to the carnival, which over time varied from place to place. In some locations, particular phases of the carnival ritual coincided with the annual slaughter of certain animals, which took on symbolic meaning. In others, specific animals were ritualistically executed. A popular example of the latter is the rooster, especially in the area that straddles southeastern France and northwestern Italy. In some cases both the slaughter of certain animals and ritual execution of others were practiced. With time, certain factions or groups celebrated their own symbolic animals (or other symbols) simultaneously. Special foods were prepared and associated with certain aspects of the carnival. There were various forms of the Maypole (sometimes in May since some carnivalesque rituals were celebrated in spring). There was

Cockaigne, the mythical land of plenty and overindulgence, as well as the tree of plenty or "tree of Cockaigne." The list is extensive.

Of the various secondary symbols, especially as one looks back in time, by far the most prevalent and most important were groups of masked figures, referred to simply as *masks*, who participated in the revelry. The importance of the mask was such that in certain instances it shared qualities with the Carnival King. It is recorded that in a few places in Italy, for example, the Carnival King was represented as a mask (Toschi 1976:130). We must therefore not be too rigid in our definition of the mask as a secondary ritual symbol, since in some cases it took on dominant qualities.

Both Toschi (1976:170) and Walter (2006:74-75), using different sources, trace the etymology of the word "mask" and come to the same conclusion. Although the Indo-European root may be difficult to establish, both scholars point to the use of the medieval *talamasca*, of pre-Gallic or Germanic origin. *Talamasca* refers to a masked figure, used in the context of carnival celebrations. Studying the European carnival, it becomes clear that during the liminal period, the suspension of cosmic order included the suspension of the principles that separated this life from the afterlife, matter from spirit, natural from supernatural. Hence, "the root of *mask* seems to be pre-Indo European, designating the spirits and creatures of the Otherworld who reveal themselves to humans at certain times of the year" (Walter 2006:75). A clear example of the vestiges of this phenomenon is to be found in Halloween traditions, derivative of the Celtic *Samhain*, a holiday that "might best be defined as November's Carnival." "This is the time when the beings of the Otherworld have temporary permission to visit the living and is also the moment when the living gain furtive access to the Otherworld" (Walter 2006:35, 37).

How were these otherworldly beings depicted in the masks? In the first edition of Toschi's *Le origini del teatro italiano* (1955:112-209) there are scattered 27 drawings and photographs of carnival masks, from extreme southern to extreme northern Italy.[4] Most striking are the photographs of ancient masks from various museums, with their horrific and grotesque features. Very often in the symbolism of primary cultures, the unnatural signals the supernatural. The unnatural characteristics of the carnival masks consist primarily in the grotesque combinations of human, animal, and sometimes even vegetative forms, which signify their otherworldliness.

> The factors or elements of culture may be recombined in numerous, often grotesque ways, grotesque because they are arrayed in terms of possible or fantasised rather than experienced combinations—thus a monster disguise may combine human, animal, and vegetable features in an "unnatural" way. . . . In other words, in liminality people "play" with the elements of the familiar and defamiliarize them. Novelty emerges from unprecedented combinations of familiar elements. (Turner 1982:27)

The progression of images presented in the plates of Toschi's book visually illustrates how the grotesque and zoomorphic characteristics of these ancient masks were transmitted to carnival and theatrical masks throughout the ages and into modern times. The "demonic" nature of their grotesque qualities, in the context of Christianity, will be addressed below.

Within the context of prehistoric agricultural/fertility rites, Toschi presents a plausible hypothesis, to explain why the masks were originally an important part of the celebrations:

> In order to generate a new plant, the seed must spend a considerable length of time underground. There, in the darkness of the underworld, dwell the regenerative powers, the subterranean divinities, demons, ancestral spirits, who—on the prophetic day which begins the new year and the eternal return of the productive cycle, invoked by the proper rituals—appear on earth and exercise their powers. (1976:167)

The masks' ability to dwell on earth was made possible by the liminality inherent in the ritual. Being otherworldly and not part of the community's social order, their function as ritual symbols seems to be rooted primarily in the sensory pole. Untethered by the social norms, which defined the ideological pole, they figured prominently in the revelry. In recent centuries, in villages throughout Europe, masked members of the community, often young men, would participate in that most carnivalesque behavior, the prank.

Toschi describes the carnival custom in the Trentino area of northern Italy, wherein masked figures were unleashed to wreak havoc in the villages. Their favorite pranks involved stealing food, and they were wont to stealthily enter homes to raid the kitchens and larders (1953:60-61). Once again, Toschi hypothesizes on the reason for associating the masks with merriment and revelry, based on his previously mentioned theory, concerning the importance of the masks as symbols of subterranean forces and their influence on the sleeping seeds. The goal is to keep them happy, as they participate in the propitiatory rite of a new agricultural cycle. "These rites are governed by a magical principal: the greater the mirth and the more the jubilation is unrestrained, then the more the crops will grow and the year will bring prosperity for the community" (1976:220).

The Roman Saturnalia

There is much evidence to indicate that carnival rites began at a time when Indo-European societies were based on early agrarian, tribal structures. This evidence includes archaeological, anthropological, iconographic, linguistic, and textual. In the context of primary cultures, as mentioned above, the social structure often reflects and is linked to cosmological order. Collective rites of passage are intrinsically connected with the work of the community and their function is to promote and increase the fertility of crops and to ensure the proper succession of the seasons. Each member of the community is obliged to participate. "In tribal societies, liminality is often functional, in the sense of being a special duty or performance *required* in the course of work or activity" (Turner 1982:52, emphasis in the original).

Over time, as tribes began to form villages and eventually some villages grew into towns and cities, the individual's as well as the community's relation to the rite began to change as well. Rural communities tended to maintain a closer connection to agrarian realities than did urban communities. Even within the social structure of a given village, not all members of the community (craftsmen and builders, for example) were directly involved with agricultural production. Social relationships based on moieties, clans, and/or totemic kinship (to name some of the possibilities found in primary cultures) began to change and be dominated more by place of birth (villages and urban neighborhoods), family lineage, and economic situations. Societies became less egalitarian and more stratified, based on wealth and power.

As tribal and early agrarian societies transformed into modern, post-industrial revolution societies, the liminal aspect of rites transformed as well. Using the suffix –oid (from Greek –eidos, meaning "resembling"), Turner coined the term *liminoid* for those activities or things that maintain vestiges of the liminal, but were no longer a required part of collective rites of passage. Activities that may be termed *liminoid* are not obligatory and are related more to a notion of play or leisure, rather than with work (1982:55). The process of rites moving historically from liminal to *liminoid* is a continuum and Turner identifies the Roman period as transitional:

> *Liminoid phenomena* flourish in societies with "organic solidarity," bonded reciprocally by "contractual" relations, and generated by and following industrial revolution, though they perhaps begin to appear on the scene in city-states on their way to becoming empires (of the Graeco-Roman type) and in feudal societies. . . . (1982:53)

In Italy much of the transition from tribal to more complex societies happened under the dominion of the Romans. The Roman version of the carnival was the Saturnalia, in honor of the agricultural god Saturn. Beginning with the winter solstice in December, it was the most important of the Roman annual holidays. Turner explains that "in liminality, profane social relations may be discontinued, former rights and obligations are suspended, the social order may seem to have been turned upside down" (1982:27). "Groups or categories of persons who habitually occupy low status positions in the social structure are positively enjoined to exercise ritual authority over their superiors; and they, in turn, must accept with good will their ritual degradation. Such rites may be described as *rituals of status reversal*" (1995:167). As Rome became the center of an empire, early Latin tribal structures transformed into dichotomies of patricians and plebes, wealthy and poor, freemen and slaves. The suspension of social order during the carnival rites took on new meaning, as they worked (albeit temporarily) more to the benefit of the subalterns, at the expense (and we may assume, the annoyance) of the privileged. What could and could not happen during the liminal period began to be dictated from above, and thus began the carnivalesque tension between popular and official cultures. Under these circumstances, it is understandable that some scholars have defined the function of the Roman carnival celebrations as a form of "safety valve," helping to release some of the social tension.

During the liminality of the Saturnalia, the suspension of the social order included a permissive spirit of *licentia* and *libertas* that was marked by irreverent behavior. Specifically, for the very paternalistic Roman society, this meant suspending the supreme authority of the *pater familias*. All forms of irreverent behavior, in particular disrespect towards the father, were reflected in the *palliatae* comedies, which were only allowed during the various holidays and *ludi* periods.[5] The *palliata* mirrored and exaggerated the Saturnalian spirit of social inversion. In the history of Western comedy, the most important playwrights of the *palliata* were Plautus and Terence. Writing about Plautine comedy, Erich Segal explains that sons bettered their fathers, slaves outwitted their masters, and the gods were blasphemed. "In sum, the very foundation of Roman morality is attacked in word and deed . . . Nothing is sacred in the world of Plautus, irreverence is endemic" (1968:31). As will be demonstrated below, the various comic and irreverent performance traditions of the ancient Romans would become instrumental during the sixteenth century, in the formation of the commedia dell'arte.

Carnival in the Christian Era

By the time the western half of the Roman Empire fell (marked at ca. 475 AD), Christianity had become the state religion (as it continued to be in the eastern half, or Byzantine Empire). Having developed within the agencies of the large and powerful empire, the Roman Church continued as an integrated and powerful institution, with Latin as its official language and Rome as its center. As Europe was being Christianized, however, the Church found itself in a struggle with myriad local mythologies and practices, which were all subsumed under the category of "paganism." But paganism was an inherent part, the substratum, of the cultures of the various European peoples, not something they could easily renounce and discard. Unable to put a halt to many pagan beliefs and practices, the Church was forced to absorb and recontextualize them under the guise of Christianity. Church hagiography, for example, began to incorporate and replace local deities and mythical figures. Many saints uncannily assumed the features and/or actions of the local deities or mythological figures they eventually replaced, including at times those related to the carnival. Philippe Walter's study (2006) presents many examples of this phenomenon.[6]

Another important aspect of the process of incorporation and recontextualization of paganism was to have Christian holidays coincide with local rites. Walter identifies the eight primary carnivalesque dates or movable feasts: "These feasts . . . originally movable because they were tied to lunar cycles, have been fixed to set days as they have been integrated into the Christian calendar" (2006:74). Again taking the example of the Celtic *Samhain*, Walter explains that in 998, Odilon, the abbot of Cluny, instituted All Souls' Day on November 2. "By placing a holiday dedicated to the dead on this particular day, he diverted toward Christian worship the ancient beliefs of *Samhain*, which were thus rendered harmless, being now attached to another vision of the Beyond that offered the hope of heaven along with the threat of hell" (2006:36).

Throughout the history of Christianity, the birth of Christ was celebrated by different sects on different dates, including variously January 6, March 25, April 10, and May 29 (Walter 2006:52). In *The Battle for Christmas*, Stephen Nissenbaum quotes the Reverend Increase Mather of Boston, who "accurately observed in 1687 that the early Christians who first observed the Nativity on December 25 did not do so 'thinking that Christ was born in that Month, but because the Heathens Saturnalia was at that time kept in Rome, and they were willing to have those Pagan Holidays metamorphosed into Christian [ones]'" (1996:4).

In the calendar of the Roman Church, carnival is celebrated as part of the sequence: Christmas season, carnival, Lent, and Easter. Carnival gaiety and overindulgence was thus contrasted to and balanced by the austerity and abstinence of Lent. By juxtaposing carnival to Lent, the Church managed to contain carnival, which in essence became "one last pagan fling before embarking on the penitential rigors of the catachumen's lententide" (Le Roy Ladurie 1979:308). Within this structure, the liminal period comes to an end with incorporation back into a Christian world order. In popular celebrations, the struggle between personifications of Carnival and Lent was enacted as part of the prelude to Carnival's execution and the end of the celebrations. (See Toschi 1976:122-65.)

Even the conventional etymology of the word "carnival," believed to derive from either Latin *carne vale* (farewell to meat) or Italian *carne levare* (to remove meat) is highly suspicious. It is the opposite of what carnival is about, since gorging on meat was often part of the celebrations, and implies instead a preparation for Lent, when eating meat was traditionally prohibited. In practice, a ritual such as carnival was around long before Lent was invented. Although the true origin of the word may never be known for certain, it seems very likely that Church Fathers at some point manipulated the term to have it fit into their schema.[7]

In the process of subduing paganism, those mythological beings that could not be absorbed and transformed by hagiography were associated with demons. In fact, the notion of associating pagan deities with demons goes back to the early Church Fathers, including St. Augustine. Along with hybrid creatures and deities of classical mythology, such as the satyr, the carnival mask with its grotesque and zoomorphic features became the model for the classical icon of the Christian devil. In popular culture the masks began to be called "devils" and "demons" and were used as representations of such in sacred plays. Once the mask is informed with both its original symbolism (as part of liminal revelry) and its Christian symbolism (signaling rebellion against God and eternal damnation), it took on another level of disparate *significata*: "The demonic and the comic are joined and fused in the same character" (Toschi 1976:218).

One of the greatest examples of how the medieval mask embodied these contrasting qualities is to be found in cantos 21-23 of Dante's *Inferno*, often described as a moment of comic relief. Dante depicts a band of devils, whose names signal their grotesque and zoomorphic attributes, inherent in the masks: Eviltail, Evilclaws, Dogscratcher, Curlybeard. The zoomorphic element is enhanced poetically as Dante employs animal imagery throughout canto 22.[8] In an analysis of cantos 21-23, Christopher Kleinhenz underscores the sense of disparate *significata* when he points out that "the words and gestures of the devils are at once menacing and playful" and refers to the "two contradictory thematic currents: devilish playfulness and diabolical cunning" (1989:137-38, 140-41). As protagonist of the narrative, Dante is terrified, even as the devils are having a rollicking time, cracking jokes as they torment the souls of corrupt government officials. Virgil confronts the devils. He informs them that the journey he and Dante are on is sanctioned by God, and demands that they be allowed to continue unmolested. Not only do the devils appear to cooperate, they offer to lead the wayfarers to the next section. But later Virgil and Dante will discover that they have been tricked. Backed by divine decree, the pilgrims could not be harmed, but the devils could not help subverting Virgil's and, indirectly, divine authority with a carnivalesque prank.[9]

Turner explains that seasonal rituals of status reversals "are often accompanied by robust verbal and nonverbal behavior, in which inferiors revile and even physically maltreat superiors" (1995:167). During the Middle Ages, as the carnival continued to lose much of its original agrarian-ritual import, socioeconomic and political tensions began to play a greater defining role.

> The common folk's use of symbols and satire is obvious. In a Carnival intended as a protest against a ruling caste, ordinarily the prime satirical instrument was the Carnival dummy or effigy made to look like the enemy of the day. . . . Protected by the anonymity of masquerade, the poor led the young people's ominous house-to-house search for alms, seeking vengeance against municipal exploiters, usurers, bloodsuckers of the people. (Le Roy Ladurie 1979:319)

Examples of the extreme levels of tension and conflict that were released during traditional carnival periods are extensive. We will limit ourselves to a few key examples. In 1580, in the small French city of Romans and the surrounding area southeast of Lyons, Carnival celebrations erupted in protests and riots by factions of the tradesmen and lower classes, which resulted in bloody reprisals (Le Roy Ladurie 1979). Despite Christianity's attempt to contain the carnival period, Christmas continued to maintain its Saturnalian origins. In New England the Puritans went so far as to prohibit the celebration of Christmas, because it involved "rowdy public displays of excessive eating and drinking, the mockery of established authority, aggressive begging . . . and even the invasion of wealthy homes" (Nissenbaum 1996:5).

Liminoid Vestiges in the Figure of the *Giullare*

The Church's attempt to confine and redefine the carnival was not altogether successful. As the carnival lost its original import as an obligatory rite of passage and its original function as a propitiatory fertility rite, *liminoid* elements began to be transferred, recontextualized, and redefined. These elements continued throughout the Middle Ages in a host of carnivalesque festivals, spectacles, and performances, such as the Feast of Fools (*festa stultorum*), Easter Laughter (*risus paschalis*), and various forms of the Fool's Play (such as the French *sotie* or *sottie*). Their defining qualities were Saturnalian *licentia* and *libertas* and the inversion of social order with a satirical sting. The carnival masks took on a new role as Christian demons in sacred plays and in "interludes in medieval plays when the 'devils' would run about among the audiences, inspiring both laughter and fear" (Kleinhenz 1989:138).

The *giullare* is the medieval itinerant performer, whose name derives from the late Latin *joculator* "player." Derivations of *jocularis* and *joculator* survive in many modern European languages.[10] After the fall of the Roman Empire, formal theatres closed and theatrical plays came to an end. Most secular performance and entertainment was limited to itinerant players and relegated to the streets, town squares, and market places. Evidence suggests that this tradition preserved some forms of Roman street performance. During the Middle Ages, when the facilities of communication and travel of the Roman Empire were suspended, the *giullare* became an important figure. As they traveled from region to region, the *giullari* circulated news and culture, and helped to maintain some form of linguistic contact between the regional languages. Although there are some extant *giullare* texts, most of their activities were part of the oral tradition. Much of the information we have is gleaned from third-person accounts, chronicles, and iconography. As for their performances, it seems that in order to survive in this trade, they needed to be versatile and able to play various instruments, to sing, dance, act, tell stories, and even perform acrobatics. Activities of the *giulleria* included magic acts as well as mountebank medicine shows. (See Townsen 1976.) The more talented and often literate *giullari* were at times welcomed into courts, where some of them were maintained as court entertainers.

Turner explains "the attributes of liminality or of liminal *personae* ('threshold people') are necessarily ambiguous, since this condition and these persons elude or slip through the network of classifications that normally locate states and positions in cultural space" (1995:95). The *giullare* by his very nature was a marginalized figure. Being itinerant, he had no home, no permanent roots, no strong loyalties to any one region.[11] He was neither urban nor rural and could not be associated with a particular class. His activities straddled the line between sacred and profane, a distinction that was at the basis of medieval society. He could freely move from recounting the lives of saints to obscene songs; he could sing the praises of martyrs as easily as he could those of wine. As far as the Church was concerned, the *giullari* represented that aspect of pagan folk culture that it was never fully able to subdue. Yet the *giullari* managed to invade sacred space. They were traditionally invited to entertain at weddings, where they might sing bawdy songs; they accompanied pilgrims; and during raucous, carnivalesque celebrations, sometimes even entered churches and parodied religious observances. Throughout the Middle Ages, various decrees prohibited *giullari* from performing in a church or other sacred places. For example, in 1207 Pope Innocent III issued such a decree, targeting profane, post-Christmas performances that took place in churches, involving "monstrous masks." It seems that low-ranking—such as priests and deacons, who traditionally hailed from the lower classes—participated as well (Casagrande and Vecchio 1978:208-35, 35n.91).

The entire Church hierarchy, from illustrious Church Fathers and theologians down to ordinary preachers, cast the *giullari* in a very bad light. Their activities were relegated to the level of drinking and gambling. Their exaggerated, *liminoid* speech and gesticulations, all of which indicated folly and madness, were to be avoided, especially by preachers. They were "cursed by God and dangerous to men." Their spiritual deformity was likened to monstrous animals. Because their performances sometimes entailed wearing carnival masks, demonic qualities were ascribed to them as well.[12] The life of the *giullare* was irredeemable—no former *giullare* could be admitted into the clergy. As a consequence of all the writing and preaching aimed at these performers, the Church was instrumental in defining the figure of the medieval *giullare* as marginalized and profane (Casagrande and Vecchio 1978:207-34).[13] As we will see, much of this will change in the thirteenth century with the establishments of mendicant orders, who, in an ironic twist of history, began to share the *giullari*'s space in the streets and piazzas.

Many qualities of the ritual symbols associated with the ancient carnival, particularly that of the Lord of Misrule, were transposed to the figure of the medieval *giullare*. Elements of the carnival's liminality endured in his activities and in his speech. The *giullare*, like the fool in the Fool's Play (a role which he often performed), "is allowed to speak the truth if he covers it with the mask of his madness" (Arden 1980:67). This character with the license to speak his mind was crystallized in the image of the court jester, and later brought to literary heights by Shakespeare's fools. From the popular perspective the *giullare* as the Lord of Misrule was not bound by the interdicts of the normal social order. This aspect of the *giullare* endures in the icon of the Joker in English playing cards, the wild card of the pack. And as an entertainer and performer in the various carnivalesque festivities, the *giullare* took on some of the symbolism and functions of the ancient carnival masks, which he sometimes wore. Like the mask, he was associated with the sensory pole: carnivalesque indulgence in eating, drinking, sex, and gaiety.

Liminoid Vestiges in the Commedia dell'Arte

During the high Renaissance, in the Veneto area of northeastern Italy, various performance trends came together, merging with new attitudes towards contracts and professionalism that would lead to the first commedia dell'arte companies, formed towards the middle of the sixteenth century. The commedia represents an extraordinary blend of oral and literary performance traditions, coming from both low and high cultures. Although scholarly attention is typically focused on the great companies that played in prestigious theatres and courts around Europe, a more complete picture encompasses "what might be called the circumambient 'culture' of the commedia dell'arte, extending from the court performer to the piazza mountebank." There was a continual cross-fertilization between the many performance modes: "stand-up performers joined organized companies, professional actors significantly influenced dilettantes, and company actors . . . published and probably also performed short printed works" (Henke 2002:2, 6).

The influence of the Roman *palliata* is enormous and well documented. The discovery of sixteen Plautine plays by Nicholas Trevirius in 1429 represents one of the greatest literary inputs into all Renaissance comedy. In Italy Trevirius' discovery sparked the tradition of Erudite Comedy, whereby men of letters, such as the historian and political writer, Nicolò Machiavelli, tried their hand at translating or rewriting *palliata* comedies, or writing original plays in the *palliata* style. (The influence of Plautus' *Menaechmi* on Shakespeare's *A Comedy of Errors*, is an example of how this tradition was passed on from Italy along with the Renaissance.) This humanist literary tradition was clearly rooted in the carnival and, as Toschi points out, records indicate these plays were staged mostly during the carnival period and other popular holidays (1953:56). The nascent commedia dell'arte absorbed *palliata* plots and storylines from Erudite Comedy, which was popular at the time. The three primary categories of *palliata* characters were the *senex* (old man), *juvenes* (youths), and *servi* (slaves). These became the *vecchi* (old men), *innamorati* (young lovers), and *zanni* (servants) of the commedia. The spirit of Saturnalian irreverence and subversion was passed on from the *palliata* to the commedia as well.

There is also evidence that suggests a continuum between forms of Roman performance traditions and the commedia dell'arte, via the oral tradition of the *giulleria*. Among the scholars who believe this are classicists. Richard C. Beacham argues that the

> mimetic expression which had originally engendered the Roman theatre continued to find an outlet in the activity of strolling players, jesters, mimes, and mountebanks, whose existence in the early medieval period is documented throughout Europe. Italy seems in particular to have been noted for its mimes and actors. . . . (1991:199-200)

With regard to the commedia, Beacham contends that "its striking resemblance to earlier popular drama makes it difficult indeed to doubt the survival of an ancient craft" (1991:200). In her investigation of Roman *mime*, a popular form of street performance, Elaine Fantham notes striking similarities with the commedia. The typical mime troupe was led by an *Archimimus*, whose role is very much akin to the *capocomico*, or leading actor, of the commedia company. And "like *Commedia dell'arte* these performances were largely improvisational with a plot outline devised by the *Archimimus*, who would roughly assign dialogue sequences (scenes) for the other players to *ad lib*" (1989:154-55).

In many ways the variety of performance modes of the *giulleria* represents one of the biggest inputs into the commedia, and Dario Fo is particularly interested in the transitional period between the medieval *giulleria* and the beginning of the commedia dell'arte (1987:98). One of the key elements in the formation of the commedia was the Venetian *buffoni*, whose performances encompassed a wide variety of modes and techniques, in the tradition of the *giulleria*.[14] But unlike the medieval *giullari*, the original *buffoni* mostly hailed from the artisan class (Henke 2002:55). It could be argued that the emergence of a class of merchants and craftsmen was the most important socio-economic development that led to the Renaissance, and it continued to be a primary force of change throughout the period. This new class began to compete with the nobility for wealth and power, offered hope for social mobility, and brought together various elements of low and high culture. The *buffoni* were mostly craftsmen and artisans, who moonlighted as entertainers. Often their stage names, such as Taiacalze, "stocking cutter," referred to their trades. Playing solo or in small groups, they performed in piazzas, and provided comic sketches at aristocratic parties and during the intermezzi of plays. "When organized companies emerged in the mid-sixteenth century, *buffone*-type actors were incorporated into the troupes, usually as the *zanni* character, and were largely responsible for their success" (Henke 2002:2, 55).

In Italian the word for "mask" (*maschera*) refers also to the stock characters of the commedia dell'arte. Regardless of whether the actor physically wore a mask or not, *maschera* refers to the stock character's iconic, exaggerated, and often predictable qualities and features.[15] Originally, the more exaggerated and comic characters, namely the *zanni* and the *vecchi* (sometimes grouped together as *parti ridicoli*), wore masks. (Later some of the masks were replaced with white powder.) Toschi convincingly argues that the grotesque zoomorphic masks of the *zanni* and *vecchi* characters of the early commedia derived from the carnival.[16] In the first edition of *Origini*, he juxtaposes various "demonic carnival masks" from northern Italy to "the oldest masks of Arlecchino, with clearly diabolic characteristics" (1955:192-93).[17] The similarities are striking: The classic commedia masks continued the bizarre human and animal combinations. Arlecchino's mask, for example, is often endowed with feline features that may include whiskers, while Il Magnifico/Pantalone's is suggestive of barnyard fowl, complete with beak and sometimes even feathers. These zoomorphic qualities were reflected in the stylized movements of the characters as well.[18]

In a chapter dedicated to "Venetian *buffoni*," Robert Henke analyzes extant texts that provide invaluable evidence to the manner and style of their performances (2002:50-68). These poems evince an irrefutable continuation of the carnival-mask heritage, as they entail descents into the underworld and encounters with demons. For example, *Il sogno di Caravia* (Caravia's dream), published in 1541, is a poem in octaves celebrating the protocommedia *buffone*, Zuan Polo. Alessandro Caravia, the author and a good friend of Zuan Polo, imagines that the recently deceased *buffone* comes to him in a dream. He tells of his visit to heaven where, with carnivalesque satire, he criticizes corruption, including that of the Church. He is consigned to hell, accompanied by the devil Farfarel. "Zuan Polo then literally clowns his way through hell, and it is here that Caravia gives some detailed portraits of his old friend's performance repertoire." He later meets his friend Taiacalze, and together they have the demons roaring with laughter, continuing the fear/mirth motif of carnival devils. At one point the *buffoni*'s peformance "shifts to a zoomorphic register, as the buffoni move through an impressive litany of bestial faces" (2002:59-60).

Communitas

As Victor Turner explains, the social structure of a community is comprised of individuals who have been conditioned to assume specific, segmentalized, social roles, including gender, status, age divisions, affiliations with various groups, etc. (1982:46). During a liminal period, the suspension of social order comprehends the suspension of individualized social roles, resulting in a shared sense of equality and connectedness he terms *communitas*, "a bond uniting people over and above any social bonds" (1974:47). *Communitas* is a relationship between members of a community that are in a state of equality, resulting from the leveling of social differences, during a liminal period. In the history of the carnival, the phenomenon of *communitas* changed along with the transformation from tribal to modern social structures, from liminal to *liminoid*. With time, as societies became more stratified and carnival became more of an outlet and a symbol of social tension, the sense of *communitas* was limited to the subalterns. Thus, during the medieval and Renaissance periods (of great interest to Dario Fo), carnival and carnivalesque celebrations provided a moment of unity and solidarity for the lower classes.

As the carnival was transformed from an obligatory, religious, agrarian rite to a raucous pre-Lenten celebration (and eventually to a mirthful masquerade), the ritual symbols and their import were transformed as well. "In liminality is secreted the seed of the liminoid, waiting only for major changes in the sociocultural context to set it agrowing into the branched 'candelabra' of manifold liminoid cultural genres" (Turner 1982:44). During the medieval-Renaissance period, the sense of liminality remained strong, as the meanings contained in the primordial carnival ritual symbols were transmitted to myriad *liminoid* manifestations. For the purposes of this study, we have focused on a limited number of these *liminoid* vestiges. More than the actual, flesh-and-blood performer, the icon of the *giullare*, as joker, jester, and Lord of Misrule, is one of the more potent and significant symbols of the carnivalesque. As symbols of temporary liminal contact with the otherworld, the zoomorphic carnival masks were transmitted to the *parti ridicoli* of the commedia dell'arte. And of course, the related *liminoid* festivities and performances are pertinent to our investigation.[19] Both the *giullari* and the masks were redefined by the Church, in an attempt to relegate them to Christian hell, resulting in residual tension between indigenous and official cultures. With this background in mind, we are now ready to take a close look at how the *liminoid* elements of the carnivalesque function in Fo's theatre and how they interact with the historical frame.

Notes

1. Often in primary, agrarian cultures, there is a notion that something must be sacrificed and "given back" to the earth.

2. Turner borrows the distinction of sign and symbol from Carl Jung. He makes it clear however that he is in total disagreement with notion that "the collective unconscious is the main formative principle in ritual symbolism" (1967:26).

3. Cross-culturally a similar function is performed by the ritual clown in Hopi culture, who is at liberty to criticize the community (Towsen 1976:9).

4. The plates in Toschi 1955 are inserted between the numbered pages. Although the second edition (1976), cited in this study, does not have any of the original plates, it does conveniently retain the pagination of the first edition.

5. The *palliata* were most likely influenced by other farcical forms, such as the Greek *phlykes* and the Oscan *Atellanae*.

6. Walter suggests that Rabelais, in a manner of speaking, reverses the process, by having Gargantua's birth coincide with St. Blaise's day and taking on some of the saint's pre-Christian qualities (2006:17).

7. For possible etymologies, see Baroja (1979:33-42) and Walter (2006:21-29). Walter presents evidence for a possible derivation from the ancient Italic goddess Carna.

8. Dante uses the human/beast combination in demonic figures throughout the *Inferno*. Toschi mentions the figure of Curlybeard (Barbariccia) in carnival celebrations, and in seventeenth-century popular literature (1976:176-77, 262).

9. In Germany, Austria, and the Friuli region of northern Italy, demonic masks, complete with horns and long tongues, known as Krampus (from the German *krampen* "claw"), were part of Christmas celebrations. Their role was to scare children into good behavior. "Europe once had a roster of Christmas rascals like Krampus, many with pagan roots. And Yule was a lot like today's Halloween." Today Krampus is making a comeback in Austria (Silver 2009:np).

10. During the Middle Ages, various forms of the word "*giullare*" were used almost interchangeably, along with other names for these performers, such as *histriones* and "mime." English borrowed the French *jongleur* because in English the word became restricted in meaning to "juggler." For this study we will employ the Italian *giullare* (pl. *giullari*) and *giulleria* for the "*giullare* tradition."

11. Though there certainly were female *giullari*, for simplicity's sake, we will refer to the classic icon of the male *giullare*, jester, fool, etc.

12. An illumination from the fourteenth-century *Térence des Ducs* depicts a performance by masked *giullari* (Beacham 1991:201).

13. Casagrande and Vecchio (1978) provide many examples and excerpts from twelfth-century ecclesiastical literature.

14. The Italian satirist, Pietro Aretino, describes a solo performance in Venice by the *buffone*, Cimador (Richards and Richards 1990:24-25). The plot, which entails a porter cuckolding a senile old husband, is reminiscent of a typical scenario of the Roman mime (Fatham 1989:154-55).

15. The tradition of a comic actor playing the same *maschera* was passed on from the commedia to variety theatre in the eighteenth and nineteenth centuries. Charlie Chaplin and Buster Keaton are two illustrious examples of actors who hailed from variety theatre and played the *maschere* they created in their films.

16. For more on carnival elements in the *maschere* of the commedia dell'arte, see Holm 1991.

17. The Franco-Germanic Hellequin/Harlequin (It. Arlecchino) has its origin in a pagan figure of the otherworld. He appears as a being of the underworld in Adam Hale's *Jeu de la feuilée*, first performed in 1276. Among Dante's devils, one is named Alichino.

18. Fo discusses the zoomorphic features of the commedia masks in 1987:27-28. In Mark's documentary (1984), Fo demonstrates the stylized bird movements of Il Magnifico.

19. For a discussion of how Fo adapted elements from the Roman *palliata* and the medieval *sottie*, see Scuderi 2000a.

Chapter Five

The Carnival Frame and Zoomorphic Symbolism

A cursory overview of Fo's early years as a performer in the 1950s demonstrates that his roots are firmly in popular theatre. He brought his earliest experiences with the *fabulatori* to the *Poer nano* radio show. His first professional stage experiences were with actors Franco Parenti and Giustino Durano, in I Dritti (The Uprights).[1] This work in the cabaret-style *avanspettacolo* (curtain raiser) gave him direct experience with the greater vaudeville tradition. While playing with I Dritti, he had the opportunity to study with the great French mime, Jacque Lecoq. He also met his future wife and collaborator, Franca Rame, who grew up in a family of popular performers. From Franca and the Rame family he learned a great deal about popular theatre, farces, and the art of improvising on a scenario, a defining technique of the commedia dell'arte that he incorporated into his *giullarata*.

Gradually Fo came to understand how all the popular traditions he was exposed to early on were related. He realized the connection between the verbal art of his first important influence, the *fabulatori*, and that of the medieval *giullari*. The art of storytelling, so essential to his epic theatre, reached heights of artistic genius with his one-man show, the *giullarata*. Thus, for example, "Cain and Abel," which Fo attributes to the *fabulatori*, was introduced in *Poer nano* and later became a sketch in *Mistero buffo*. His experience with the *avanspetacolo* led to an exploration of Italian variety theatre, and later a book on one of its masters, Totò (Fo 1991a). He comprehended how the commedia dell'arte developed and existed in dialectic with popular forms of performance. Even at the end of its centuries' run, as it started to lose its appeal and connection with audiences, the commedia informed various types of *teatro minore*, such as clowning, vaudeville, the French schools of mime (including those of Marcel Marceau and Jacque Lecoq), and the English pantomime. This process happened primarily during the eighteenth and nineteenth centuries, late enough for it to be well documented. Fo's passion for *teatro minore* led to *Throw the Lady*

Out (*La signora è da buttare*, first produced in 1967), a show he and Rame developed and performed together with professional circus clowns. The process of accumulating experience with popular forms and studying the history of Italian/European theatre allowed Fo to develop his own popular-derived theatre, with its intricate framing and complexities. In later years, his knowledge of historical stagecraft would be put to use in the various productions of Rossini operas throughout Europe. In these productions, Fo directed, choreographed, designed sets and costumes, and cleverly employed various theatrical techniques of past centuries.

The Carnival Manifesto

The 1960s represent an important period in the development of Fo's theatre. It is during this time that he matured as a playwright. Within Italy his and Rame's popularity was greatly boosted by their brief stint in television. Later, as they successfully toured outside of Italy, other European companies began to perform his plays. During the turbulent '60s he began to explore various forms of popular performance, such as traditional music in *Ci ragiono e canto* and circus clowning in *Throw the Lady Out*. He also initiated his study of medieval history and culture, which culminated with the development of his masterpiece, *Mistero buffo* in 1969.[2] Fo always had a penchant for the grotesque and the carnivalesque, especially with relation to farce, and elements suggesting the carnival can be found in early plays (Holm 2000:126, 134). With exposure to studies such as those of Toschi and Bakhtin, he gained great insight into the carnival tradition, and was able to define and develop his carnival frame.

Isabella, Three Sailing Ships and a Conman could be considered a manifesto of Fo's intention to contextualize his theatre within a greater carnival frame and give it a new direction. *Isabella* is firmly framed by the carnival. Bent Holm points out that from the opening of the curtain, the carnival is signaled by a greasy pole (the tree of Cockaigne), and it is soon made clear by the opening dialogue that the play takes place during the carnival period. As was mentioned, an actor, played by Fo, has been condemned by the

Inquisition. There is a chance that he may receive a pardon and he is granted the opportunity to perform a play. Using the gallows as a stage, he performs a play about Columbus in order to delay his execution. At the end, the actor is executed, much like the Carnival King, by a carnival mask—Pulcinella, dressed in black. His final performance could be taken as Carnival's last testament (Holm 2000:133-35). Fo, who in his epic-theatre style never fully gets into character, is simultaneously Fo/condemned actor, and Fo/Columbus. As Columbus he is the intellectual who tries to play within the power structure. As the executed actor, he is the Carnival King.

First, it should be noted that the play itself was a milestone in the maturation of his playwriting. It was his first full-length performance in a historical setting, and he took the opportunity to apply the reversal in a more sophisticated and multifaceted way than in his earlier stories or variety sketches. Although in the Anglophone world it is not considered alongside his more popular plays, *Isabella* broke box-office records in Italy. Other European companies put on their own productions, including one in Sweden in 1965 and one in Paris in 1971 (Mitchell 1999:77). Fo considers the play important as we can discern from his own revival in Valencia in 1992, during the quincentennial celebrations of Columbus' voyage. More importantly, his masterpiece, *Johan Padan*, which also takes place during Columbus' voyages, has many echoes of *Isabella*.

Whereas Fo's previous *giullarate* had been comprised of various individual sketches, *Johan Padan* was his first *giullarata* that consisted of one long story, with a duration of over two hours. The last song in *Isabella* introduces the performance on video (1992c). In the prologue, he explicitly introduces *Johan Padan* as a continuation of *Isabella*, and explains that he is using the same backdrop that he had painted for the older play. He gives as background some of the historical information about the activities of Spanish King and Queen (such as expelling the Jews) that was treated in *Isabella*. The two plays are also closely linked by indexical framing. In a flashback in *Isabella*, Columbus is the only sailor able to foresee a deadly storm that is about to come (1966:80-84). Although at his trial an accuser tries to attribute his prescience to witchcraft, this foreknowledge is presented as an example of Columbus' extraordinary seamanship. Columbus retorts, "And yet it is only intelligence. Stupid people are always afraid of new things" (84). Similarly, in the fabular *Johan Padan*, predicting deadly storms is presented in terms of magic and witchcraft. It becomes an important leitmotif and is repeated three times: In the beginning Johan's sorceress girlfriend in Venice predicts a storm and teaches him how to do it (1992e:6-7); Johan predicts a deadly storm, which greatly raises his status among his cannibal captors (55-58); and finally, after the climactic battle with the Spanish, Johan and his *Indios* delay releasing their vengeful prisoners until he is sure there is a storm waiting for them (108-12). The two plays are linked by other motifs, such as a description of the worthless booty Columbus brought back from his first voyage. Having failed in his attempts to sail to Asia and bring back gold and spices, in both plays Columbus merely returns with a few natives, some parrots, and not much else of monetary value (1966:54; 1992e:13).[3] By signaling the importance of *Isabella* in his oeuvre, Fo underscores its key position in the development of his theatre.

By the end of the 1960s, with Isabella and with the development of the *giullarata* mode of performance, Fo made clear his intentions to be associated with two of the most important symbols of the carnival: the Lord of Misrule and the *giullare*, informing himself and his theatre with *liminoid* qualities. Turner writes,

> the solitary artist *creates* the liminoid phenomena, the collectivity *experiences* collective liminal symbols. This does not mean that the maker of *liminoid* symbols, ideas, images, etc., does so *ex nihilo*; it only means that he is privileged to make free with his social heritage in a way impossible to members of culture in which the liminal is to a large extent the sacrosanct. (1982:52 emphasis in the original)

Fo's theatre functions liminally under the suspension of social order, as carnival elements run throughout many of his plays.

With *Mistero buffo*, under the umbrella of liminality, he begins his re-presentation of history. In the text we find this explication of popular medieval iconography, which was presented as slides for the performance (and are reproduced in the text):

Here is a sequence of buffooneries [jests or pranks], that is, a sort of preparation for ironic-grotesque performances, in which the folk, dressed up and disguised, participated.
These were the common folk. You can see them. This one is dressed up as a *mammuttones*. What is a *mammuttones*? It is a very ancient mask, half goat and half devil. In Sardinia still today the folk, during certain feasts . . . go around with masks that are very similar to the ones we are seeing in these images. You see that almost all of them are devils. Here, this one is a *giullare*, the figure of the joker,[4] the madman, a folk allegory. Here is another devil, and another . . . . (1977b:12-13)

In this passage he brings together important *liminoid* symbols of the medieval carnival, such as masks with zoomorphic and demonic features, and the *giullare*. He connects the zoomorphic mask to a living folk tradition. He defines the *giullare* as a *liminoid* icon: "a folk allegory," embodying the satirical sting of the *sot* or madman and the license inherent in the concept of a "wild card," that is not bound by rules or norms. In his performances, Fo often embodies the carnival-charged *liminoid* symbol of the *giullare* and the fool. His brand of satirically charged farce, shares many elements with carnivalesque spectacles of the Middle Ages, such as the various forms of the Fool's Play. A primary reason that explains Fo's interest in the medieval/Renaissance period is the way in which official culture viewed laughter as an essential part of carnival and carnivalesque traditions:

> Laughter in the Middle Ages remained outside all official spheres of ideology and outside all official strict forms of social relations. An intolerant one-sided tone of seriousness is characteristic of official medieval culture. . . . Early Christianity had already condemned laughter. Tertullian, Cyprian, and John Chrysostom preached against ancient spectacles, especially against mime and the mime's jests and laughter. John Chrysostom declared that jests and laughter were not from God but from the devil. (Bakhtin 1984:73)

82   Chapter Five

References to grotesque lower-body functions, in a Bakhtinian register, run throughout Fo's works and create a pervasive spirit of the carnival. Even in his autobiography, for example, he uses this register to underscores the comic abilities of his grandfather, nicknamed Bristin, (hot pepper seed), an accomplished raconteur. On an outing with his vegetable cart, Bristin sends a poor woman into a fit of uncontrollable laughter: "'Oh God, enough Bristin'! a large woman, holding her belly, implored him. 'I'll wet myself'! And with that, she lifted her skirt, swept it back, revealing a long rivulet of pee on the cobblestones" (2002:49).

Very often, however, what may seem to be random madcap humor and/or scenes involving lower-body capers have specific historical roots in carnival and other traditions. As an example, we may refer back to Fanfani's belly swelling in such a way that he is mistaken for a pregnant woman. The same motif appears in *Can't Pay*, when Antonia and Margherita try to pump up the unconscious brigadier of the *carabinieri* with oxygen in order to revive him. They mistakenly use hydrogen, and cause his stomach to swell up. "Now we got a policeman pregnant"! (1974a:79). This theme is taken directly from carnival cults involving the bean, "the Carnival food par excellence, given that it causes the stomach to swell and can therefore make a man resemble a pregnant woman. There are a great number of Carnival brotherhoods that find amusement in the ambiguity brought on by this bloating" (Walter 2006:27). During the liminal period, the ambiguity created by confusing of gender is part of the suspension of social roles that create the sense of equality and *communitas*. In both examples given from Fo's plays, the false pregnancy functions to satirize an authority figure.

The false pregnancy assumes even greater proportions in *Can't Pay!*, a play in which "the carnivalesque is important from the very first moment" (Walsh 1985:213). The play zeros in on a specific socio-economic situation of Italy in 1974, as working-class families could no longer cope with rising food prices. The reaction was a grass-roots movement called *autoriduzione dei prezzi* (self-reduction of prices), whereby shoppers would pay what they felt was a fair price. (Some people even resorted to outright stealing from supermarket shelves.) In *Can't Pay*, women are transporting stolen food by stashing it under their coats, in such a way as to look pregnant. In an attempt to explain to a police brigadier why all the neighborhood women suddenly look pregnant, Antonia explains that they are celebrating the cult of their local patron saint, "Eulalia of the Large Belly," who miraculously became pregnant at the age of seventy. As the play progresses, the tale of the saint becomes more and more bizarre and leads to a series of zany gags.

> Little matter that [Antonia] distorts completely the historical Eulalia, a virgin martyr under Diocletian. Twelve-year-old Eulalia was supposed to have trampled on sacrificial cake proffered her and spat at her examining judge. It is her antiauthoritarianism to which Antonia no doubt responds, and the bogus cult remains curiously true to the original saint. (Walsh 1985:217)

Thus, what seems to be simply an outrageous and hilarious fabrication is actually a carnivalesque inversion of a chapter of Catholic hagiography. Furthermore, the original story of Eulalia is encoded with a sense of rebellion that supports the actions of Antonia and her neighbors.

Zoomorphic Symbolism

From an anthropological perspective, Fo sees elements of universality in the features of the ancient ritual masks that hark back to a primordial time that is, to some extent, beyond the full reach of our knowledge. He explained this to me in an interview:

> Not only are there masks from popular traditions that are still found today in the countryside of the South [southern Italy], among the Arabs, among the Turks, among the Persians, among the Chinese, and so on, in which you can see very well that they have ancient roots that sometimes go beyond those roots that we are aware of. Even earlier, they were part of fertility rites, for example, and they were sometimes part of taboo. (1993)

He draws much of his grotesque imagery from ancient masks. "*Cracokis* is that hunched-back mask that comes from Turkey and from Persia . . . *Cracokis* is then grafted onto some of the Roman masks, who were originally Asian to begin with" (1993). As he explained to me that hunchbacks seem to have been much more prevalent in former times, he spontaneously demonstrated the use of the grotesque to parody authority: "The only one left is Andreotti" (1993), referring to one of the most powerful men in Italian politics. This imagery is akin to the satire of the medieval carnival, when "the prime satirical instrument was the Carnival dummy or effigy made to look like the enemy of the day" (Le Roy Ladurie 1979:319). Fo continued, "The hunch-back is a strange tradition, because he who has a hunched back must also be shrewd" (1993).

In "Phallicthropic Harlequin"—originally in *Mistero buffo* and again in *Hellequin, Harlekin, Arlecchino*—Arlecchino drinks a love potion (of course intended for someone else) and grows an enormous penis. Using mime, Fo's Arlecchino tries to disguise his overgrown appendage in various ways, such as pretending it is a cat or a baby. This is one way that Fo tries to inject some of the carnivalesque liminality he feels was lost in the commedia, as it was sweetened in later centuries.

> Arlecchino in his origins was a character who very much resembled the wild man of the forest, brutal, violent, rude, trivial, obscene. Then he gradually transformed during the seventeenth and eighteenth centuries. By the nineteenth, century he had become a mask that was sentimental, often simply clownish, without his original edge. (1993)

Fo sees the grotesque as a device "that dismantles the workings of a bogus reality" (1992a:35). As Bakhtin observes, one of the most ancient forms of the grotesque is the combination of human and animal traits (1984:316), characteristic of the liminal carnival masks and their *liminoid* continuation in the *giulleria* and in the commedia. His *giullarate* are richly encoded with zoomorphic imagery, often in conjunction with reference to the bodily lower stratum. Key sketches to illustrate the point are "The Birth of the Peasant" from *Mistero buffo*, which explains how the peasant was born from a donkey. In the sketches that comprise *Obscene Fables*, we note "The Butterfly-Mouse," a reference to female genitalia, and "Lucio and the Ass," which involves a human-to-animal metamorphosis, with the donkey as a symbol of the male sex drive.

In *Johan Padan* Fo uses animals to create a symbolic code to convey and underscore various things, including: the fascination of the Europeans with the New World; the sense of unfamiliarity between two different cultures; and the bestial ways in which human beings treat each other. When the Europeans arrive in the New World, they encounter new animals, such as flying fish, pumas, turkeys, and iguanas. In performance, the elaborate depictions of the New World animals, accompanied by Fo's extraordinary mime, convey Johan's utter fascination.[5] At the same time, in their ships the Europeans bring horses, donkeys, cows, and domesticated pigs, animals the Native Americans had never seen.

The inability of two ethnic groups to act humanely towards one another is represented in the way that they treat each other as animals. On the trip back to Europe, in place of animals, the ship's hold is crammed with enslaved *Indios*. As they die from the harsh and unsanitary conditions, the Europeans cut them up to use as fishing bait. Likewise the native cannibals prepare their European victims for slaughter in the same way that they prepare their turkeys. Johan describes how the natives rip the feathers out of the living turkeys to tenderize the meat. Later, his cannibal captives prepare him for eating by brutally tearing out his body hair in the same manner. In a very Bakhtinian register, Fo works in grotesque combinations to underscore the human/animal confusion. When a group of Native Americans first encounters European domesticated pigs, "they think they're another race of Christians, just a little fatter" (1992e:29). When the *Indios* first see mounted soldiers, "they are convinced that the rider and the horse are a single beast; that from the horse's body springs the torso and arms of a man" (21).

The use of animals to signal the bestial nature of humans is also found in "The Holy Jester and the Wolf of Gubbio," an episode from the *giullarata The Holy Jester Francis* (the subject of the next chapter). In this legend, Saint Francis of Assisi confronts a huge and vicious wolf that is terrorizing the area. In Fo's retelling, Francis confronts the wolf and demands an explanation for his deplorable behavior, ravaging the countryside, attacking livestock and people for the sheer pleasure of it. Fo's talking wolf (brilliantly rendered with low-pitched, raspy voice) explains that it is in his nature. The Saint launches an invective on the bestial nature of human beings, laced with Fo's Marxist-Gramscian indignation for the exploitation of the downtrodden: "This is rich! Did you think this all by yourself? (*Changes tone*) Get it? It's all a matter of nature. If you are born with this nature you can rob, rape women, slaughter, lie like a rug, kill . . ." (1999a:42). Fo's Saint Francis establishes peace and coexistence between the wolf and the local people. Later he again encounters the wolf who explains how the locals began to treat him badly and drive him away. The wolf comes to the conclusion that if a ferocious animal loses his bestial nature, no one will respect him. Francis pensively considers his error: "It's all my fault! How presumptuous of me, thinking that I could transform a wolf into a good Christian. Instead I did not understand that, first, I should try to transform Christians into good animals!" (50).

Fo often uses zoomorphic imagery to deflate pompous and authoritative figures of hegemonic power. On several occasions he reduces the Christian icon of the winged archangel to poultry. In "The Wedding at Cana," from *Mistero buffo*, the drunk (i.e. the subversive clown) drives off the solemn, authoritative angel: "I'll tear your feathers out like a chicken, one by one, even from your ass! Get back here you overgrown rooster! Get back here" (1977b:62). In "The First Miracle of the Christ Child," from *The Tale of a Tiger and Other Stories*, the spectacular appearance of an archangel scatters the shepherds' flocks. An angry shepherd vents his anger: "If only you'd go and crash into the mountain so that your halo gets rammed down to your neck, with all your feathers scattered everywhere. Turkey!" (1980:85).

In the same sketch Fo connects the magic of a child's imagination to the grotesque combinations of primordial art, such as those in carnival masks, totem poles, and the like. The child Jesus has demonstrated to the neighborhood children how he can breathe life into a bird he forged from clay and send it into flight. Now all the children delight in creating flying creatures from clay: "Then another kid makes a sausage, a salami-snake, with twelve wings in flight, no tail, twelve legs . . . Then another made a mush, a sort of cake, with a head right in the middle, no neck, beak up, and all the wings unpaired, all around. And no legs" (105).[6] Relating the images to types of food offers an added touch of the Rabelaisian.

The Cooked and the Raw

As would be expected, amongst Fo's *giullarate*, animal symbolism plays an essential role in "The Tale of a Tiger," the main sketch of *The Tale of a Tiger and Other Stories*. In the prologue Fo explains that he learned the story from an oral performer in Shanghai. "I heard this story told—more precisely, performed—for the first time four years ago, in Shanghai, in China. During this time many of these stories were told down there" (1980:5). This account of the tale's origin was part of the prologue of the performance as well (1991b). However, in an interview in 1975, Fo told a different version of how he saw this story performed in China. Amongst other inconsistencies, the tiger character was originally an old woman (1992a:298). In the time between this interview and the premiere of *Tiger*, Fo began to enact a tiger briefly as a part of his performances of *Mama's Marijuana Is the Best* (produced in 1976).[7]

Fo's invention about the origin of the tiger story is illustrative of several aspects of his framing. First, it seems important to frame "Tiger" within a living oral tradition. The fact that the story is probably Fo's invention, yet is presented as folklore, points to Gramsci's ideas on folk songs (quoted above), where he suggests that all popular songs can be considered,

> written neither by the people nor for the people, but adapted by the people because they conform to their manner of thinking and feeling . . . since that which distinguishes a popular song, in the context of a nation and its culture, is neither the artistic factor nor its historic origin, but the way in which it conceives the world and life, in contrast to official society. (Q 5, par. 156)

Continuing with Fo's prologue to "Tiger," we note that the performer speaks a local dialect and has carvinalesque-*liminoid* qualities, for he is essentially a *giullare* working within an ironic and grotesque tradition.

> Outside of official theatre, the most dynamic was the popular theatre, in the outskirts, unknown to passing tourists, a true creation of imagination, of the grotesque and the ironic.
> I don't believe that this story is still performed today as I saw it, narrated before thousands of people . . . in a meadow of the Shanghai countryside. The *fabulatore* expressed himself in the rural dialect of Shanghai, spoken by a minority. [. . .]
> That extraordinary *giullare* used the gestures of his hands and arms and the movement of his whole body, sometimes complementing and sometimes contrasting with his yells and his sounds. His words were contracted and expanded, then silence and pantomime. I understood that I was witnessing great theatre, where the protagonist was a tiger. (1980:5-6)

It becomes clear that inventing facts is part of Fo's framing process and thus part of the performance. The element of liminality is the wild card, which frees the Lord of Misrule from the conventional norms governing "facts" and grants him the *licentia* to invent.

As Fo explains, the tiger in the story is a very clear allegory, for, according to him, in Chinese culture it represents stalwartness, constancy, and perseverance. The country folk of the Shanghai area add that those who possess the tiger "can withstand to the point of holding embers in the palms of their hands, so that, when those who were panic-stricken and fled, later, regaining their courage and return, they will find those who kept the fire alive, to begin again, to reorganize and together take up the struggle" (8). As we shall see, these qualities of the tiger allegory are closely associated with a more universal spirit of the folk, which represents a force more powerful than any ideology or governing body, even a Communist one.

In Fo's tale however the figure of the tiger works at a more subtle level as well. When discussing the roots of culture, Fo at times refers to *memory* in the Jungian sense, as an innate collective memory of a distant past. With reference to the origins of music and dance, for example, he states, "I was trying to underscore the value that these roots assume even in our memory" (1987:53). It seems he intends to connect at this level with his audience's memory, by encoding his performance with primordial elements, such as carnival celebration and zoomorphic imagery. "Tiger" in particular is encoded with references to a mythological past that inform the tiger with totemic qualities that refer back to the beginnings of culture.

The tale is narrated in the first person. The unnamed protagonist, a soldier of Mao's Red Army, is wounded in the leg during the grueling, 6000-mile Long March from Jiangxi to Yan'an. His comrades leave him behind to die.[8] In order to find shelter from diluvian rains, he drags himself along, crosses a torrent, and finally takes shelter in a cave, which turns out to be the den of a tigress and her cubs. She returns carrying one cub that drowned in the floods and accompanied by another cub that nearly drowned and is too bloated to nurse. She is suffering from the pressure of lactation. A symbiotic relationship which suggests a mythological bond between human and nature begins: The soldier relieves the tiger's suffering by nursing, and she in turn nourishes him with her milk and heals his gangrenous wounds by licking them. Fo adds a little wisdom from folk medicine, explaining that "the tiger's slaver is a wonderful ointment, miraculous, a medicine" (27). Fo uses imagery that is open to Freudian interpretations. The protagonist must travel across water and enters a cave, which could imply the womb. From the tiger's perspective, she has lost a cub, and the soldier appears to take its place. The tale lends itself further to Jungian interpretations, with the cave representing the unconscious. Taking the allegory of the tiger from the prologue as an interpretive key, we understand that the soldier discovers his inner resources, including courage and perseverance.

The mythological human/nature motif continues. During the time the convalescing soldier lives with the tigress and her surviving cub, they bond and become a threesome. At one point, when he is able to walk, the soldier builds a fire and cooks some meat from the tigers' latest kill. He shares it with them, and they learn to prefer cooked meat over raw. Having discovered the delights of cooked meat, the tigers oblige the soldier to cook for them every day. When the soldier, who has tired of continuously cooking for the tigers, leaves the den to find a village, the tigers, who now long for cooked meat, follow him. The situation Fo presents is a reversal of a common Prometheus or fire-theft myth, such as the ones reported and analyzed in *The Raw and the Cooked*, Claude Lévi-

Strauss' study of Amazonian mythology (1975). The fire-theft myths explain how humans acquired fire and learned to cook from a totemic animal. In one of the most common versions, the hero is taken in by the animal, often a jaguar, who introduces him to fire and cooked meat. The hero then returns home, and a group of humans, often in the form of animals or assisted by animals, return to the jaguar's abode to steal the fire. In Lévi-Strauss' title "raw" and "cooked" refer to "nature" and "culture" respectively.

Once again, taking the symbolism he offers in the prologue, the fire for Fo is the human struggle for a better world, the most important endeavor of human culture. Considering the historical setting of the play, the struggle refers specifically to the Maoist struggle against the Nationalists and the Japanese. As we shall see, Fo extends this to include the struggle against abuses of power under communist rule.[9] In Fo's story a human imparts fire to a creature of nature, thus inverting the mythological sequence. The crux of Fo's myth is not procuring fire for humans. Instead, the soldier introduces fire (the proletarian struggle) to the tiger (human fortitude, courage, perseverance). A possible interpretation of this, from a Jungian perspective, is that the protagonist enters the unconscious and assimilates these inner resources. Inverting the mythological sequence is a clever narrative strategy, because the tigers are brought back to the humans' world and continue as characters in the story. The enacting of the tigers became a tour de force of Fo's *giullarata* performance, "not even in *Mistero buffo* did Fo create for himself such a platform for his acting talents" (Farrell 2001:215).

With the interaction of the soldier and the tigers, the human/animal bond is suggested and reinforced at various levels. On several occasions, in a comic register and with Fo's typical irony, the protagonist/narrator talks about the tigers as if they were a human family, e.g.: "But what kind of mother is she? Bringing such a young child out to wander about in the night. What will he become when he grows up? A beast!" (31). Later when the tigers catch up with the soldier in the village, they berate him for running off and he complains about having to cook all day. This interaction, in which humans and animals are conversing together with roars and words (ingeniously rendered in performance), is couched in terms of a domestic quarrel:

> When they came to a distance of about ten meters, the mother tiger started making a scene. And what a scene: "AAHHAAAA Fine gratitude! After all I did for you, even licking your wounds OOHHAAAHHHAAA I saved your life! EEOOHHAAAA I wouldn't have done it for one of my males, not even for a member of my own family. EEOOHHAAAA You ditched us there! OOHHAAHHAAA And then you taught us to eat cooked meat. Now every time EEOOHHAAHHAA that we eat raw meat we get nauseous." [. . .]
>
> And I replied: "OOHHAAAA And what did you do? I even saved your life by suckling, or else you would have burst, AHOLAHHH! And then cooking and cooking until my balls were about to pop. Eh?" [. . .]
>
> But then, as always happens when there is love in a family, we made peace. (49-50)

Placing man and tiger on the same level by having them communicating in the same language, albeit in a comic register, has mythological import. As Lévi-Strauss observed in his study of fire-theft mythology, "It is important to remember that in mythological terms there was no distinction between men and animals" (1975:113).

After peace is restored, the soldier introduces the tigers to the villagers (who must first overcome their fears). The tigers, now used to humans and ritually acculturated by the cooked meat, quickly become members of the community, moving from natural to social beings. At this point the story suggests the completion of a rite of passage: The protagonist was separated from his fellow soldiers; he passed through a period of liminality, living in a natural condition with the tigers; and he returns to the world of humans, reintegrating himself and the tigers to the community.

The tigers prove to be very useful in frightening and driving off the marauding army of Chiang Kai-shek from the protagonist's adopted community and neighboring villages. When the demand for protection becomes too great for the two tigers to fulfill by themselves, the protagonist devises a strategy. Since the enemy has learned to fear tigers and runs at the sight of them, he teaches the villagers how to imitate tigers by using masks and costumes, and simulating their movements and roars. This episode is heavily charged with meta-performance implications, because throughout the play Fo has been enacting the tigers' movements, sounds, and even their "speech," displaying his extraordinary talents for mime and *grammelot*. This meta-performance, in which Fo both enacts tigers and tells a story of people who enact tigers, is one of the most important ways he encodes his story with totemic elements that recall a primordial past. In *Manuale minimo*, he discusses the use of masks, specifically animal disguises, by prehistoric hunters:

> Anthropologists explain that first of all it serves to block the taboo. Ancient peoples . . . believed that each animal could count on a specific deity for protection. With the disguise, the hunter avoided the terrible wrath of the goat deity, for having killed one of his wards, without the permit of the counter-taboo. [. . .] The rite of disguise with animal skins and masks is linked to the culture of all the people of this earth. (1987:22)

Fo feels strongly about the importance of a people establishing a connection with their history, a point made on numerous occasions. In a chapter entitled "To Have a Revolution, You Must First Dance the Jaguar," Fo discusses the Angolan revolution:

> With the passing of time these people, who had been under Portuguese rule for more than three centuries, had lost every connection, every link with their own history, their own origins [. . .] A people without a culture has no dignity, is not concerned with its own roots, and thus has no desire to fight and free itself. The first thing this group of educated Angolans [the organizers of the revolution] had to do was try to revive their primordial rituals. One of the most important involved preparing for hunting the jaguar [sic].[10] (1987:54)

He explains how the Angolan warriors had to relearn their traditional dances that imitated the big cat's movements, in order to awaken the feline's qualities within themselves, thus making contact with their primordial roots (1987:54-55). In "Tiger" it is suggested that the villagers connect with their totemic roots and with those positive qualities embodied by the tiger.

With their tigers and their ability to simulate tigers, the villagers are very successful in driving off Chiang Kai-shek's forces, and a party official comes to congratulate them. "The folk has inventiveness and imagination like no one else on earth. Well done!" However he adds, "But now the tigers cannot be kept any longer. You have to send them back to the forest were they belong" (57). When the perplexed villagers inquire why they should send away these creatures, who are their friends and have helped and protected them, the explanation is delivered by the official in party rhetoric: "We cannot, tigers are anarchistic, they lack dialectic, we cannot assign them a role in the party. If they cannot be in the party, they cannot remain. They lack dialectic. Obey the party. Return the tigers to the forest" (57).

The people disobey and hide the tigers in their henhouses, and we are presented with yet another grotesque amalgam in a farcical register. Whereas humans learned to imitate the tigers, now, in order to fool party officials, the tigers are taught to act like chickens. "The political bureaucrat stood there a second, figured it was a 'tigered rooster,' and went away" (59). The decision is a good one, and when the Japanese invade, the tigers drive them away as well. Another party official arrives and praises the people for having disobeyed the first one, "who, among other things, was a counterrevolutionary revisionist." Nevertheless, the new official also orders the people to send the tigers back to the forest.

What? Again?

Obey the party.

Because of dialectic?

Of course! (59)

As the play continues, the pattern repeats: Another invasion by Chiang Kai-shek is thwarted by the tigers and another party official arrives to praise the people for having disobeyed the last one. He proclaims that the tigers will always remain with the people . . . but in a zoo. His extended discourse is also couched in party rhetoric. Fo's parody of ideological-political double-talk reaches a grotesque pitch: ". . . there isn't even that dimension of expressive dialectic that determines a direction that naturally starts at the vertex but that then develops into the base that gathers and refutes those which are the proposed indications" . . . (61). The official's bombastic discourse is interrupted by the appearance of the tigers, "'The TIGERRRRS!' (*Mimes a violent attack towards the officials*)," and the play ends with a tremendous roar: "EEEAAAAAAAAHHHHHHHHAAAAAAAAAA!!!" (61).

Fo had journeyed to China in 1975. "The lack of critical independence Fo displayed in the many interviews he gave on his return is startling. His glowing account of the devotion of the Chinese people for Mao and the Communist Party reads like the life of a saint in a devotional manual . . ." (Farrell 2001:160-61). Although some of Fo's misreading of the Chinese situation could be attributed to the rigid control of information about the actual situations within the country, he was later forced to recant his misplaced idealism. However, in "Tiger," Fo gives the last word to the folk and their culture. He makes it clear that the qualities of the tiger—steadfastness, constancy, and perseverance—are inherent to the folk and not to any ideology or political party.

Fo's masterpiece harkens back to the primordial imagination and the beginning of human culture. It is a play specifically informed by a sense of a mythological totemic union—the memory of the belief in supernatural beings that have both human and animal qualities. Fo's symbolism is derived from the zoomorphic masks used in prehistoric rites of passage, including those of the carnival, and continued with the masked stock characters of the commedia dell'arte. In his *giullarate*, zoomorphic symbolism plays an important and multifaceted role, and functions as part of the underlying spirit of the grotesque that informs his carnival frame.

Notes

1. The name Uprights was intended as a parody of a popular comedy group called The Hunchbacks (Farrell 2001:37).
2. In a lengthy doctoral dissertation, Simone Soriani (2007) outlines the development of Fo's one-man show, over this ten-year period.
3. This theme is much more developed in the various texts and performances of *Johan Padan*. See Scuderi 1998:59-60.
4. Fo uses *jolly*, which Italian took from "The Jolly Joker" of English playing cards.
5. In the prologue Fo underscores the historic accounts and explorers' travelogues he used to prepare the show. However, it is obvious that literary sources, such as the picaresque novel, are equally important. Fo's New World creatures are informed with a sense of the fantastic, much like in Defoe's *Robinson Crusoe* (see 1975:26).
6. Images of winged snakes, to give one example, are found in the engravings of Mississippian Civilization, such as Spiro Mound in Oklahoma, which dates c. A.D. 700-1200.
7. The inconsistency between Fo's introduction to "Tiger" and the interview was pointed out by Holm (2002:125-26). My thanks to Valeria Tasca for the information on *La marijuana*.
8. "When Brecht . . . devised a similar situation in *The Measures Taken*, also set in China, his activist accepted death rather than impede the revolution. Dario's soldier, on the other hand, refuses the 'offer' made by one of his comrades to shoot him" (Farrell 2001:213).
9. It should be noted that, although a Marxist, Fo never joined the communist party (Farrell 2001:80).
10. We can assume that by "jaguar," which is native to Central and South America, Fo intends the African "leopard."

Chapter Six

Dario Fo and *The Holy Jester Francis*

In 1995, while preparing to take *Johan Padan* to the United States, Fo suffered a stroke that impaired his eyesight and his memory. Considering his age at the time, sixty-nine, and the energy it takes to perform a one-man show for over two hours, there was concern that this may very well have been his last major solo piece. Fortunately his recovery was good (though not complete) and *Johan Padan* was not the last of his major *giullarate*. In July 1999, he premiered a new *giullarata*, *The Holy Jester Francis* (*Lu santo jullàre Françesco*), based on the life of Saint Francis of Assisi (1182-1226). This show, about one of the Western world's most beloved historical figures, was presented by Italy's most controversial and, for many, most beloved entertainers. Fo was also by now a Nobel laureate. *The Holy Jester* was received enthusiastically, and the Einaudi press immediately issued a text accompanied by a performance on video.[1] It was even deemed acceptable by the Catholic Church, as we shall see.

As the historian Franco Cardini explains, Francis "is the most popular saint of the Catholic world and one of the most famous, loved, and admired figures in the history of humanity" (1989:24). "Every generation feels the need to create 'his' version of 'his' Francis" (1989:26). One reason why the figure of Saint Francis lends itself to continuous redefinition is that the Church's official biography of this saint represents a manipulation of the transmission of history. The Church gave Saint Bonaventure (1217-1274) the authority to write the definitive, official version of Saint Francis' biography, *The Major Life of Saint Francis*. Chiara Frugoni explains,

> At the same time it was decreed, and with great efficacy, that all other biographies be destroyed. Hundreds of manuscripts disappeared, and for centuries the only Francis who could be known was that of Bonaventure and of his ingenuous interpreter, Giotto.[2] It was not until the end of the nineteenth century that

some copies of the condemned biographies were found. Historians began to discover incredible discrepancies of dates and events, giving rise to a debate, which goes on till this day. (1995:134)

What does become clear from the documentation that comes down to us is Francis' extraordinary ability to connect with the popular masses. He was a powerful communicator, who used popular language and secular techniques of public address, as well as *giullaresque* histrionics, to deliver his gentle message. The lessons and exempla he acted out were often aimed at bringing the moral lesson of a given situation into perspective. In his own lifetime he saw the order he had founded become an immense institution that would quickly extend throughout the entire Western world. The influence he exercised far exceeded the ecclesiastical sphere, for the Franciscans introduced themselves into the quotidian life of the masses to an extent which no other institution had ever before achieved.

Fo's *Giullare*

In a brief passage devoted to Saint Francis in his book *Mimesis*, Erich Auerbach underscored Francis' extraordinary power of performance: "He forced his inner impulse into outer forms; his being and his life became public events . . . everything he did was a scene. And his scenes were of such power that he carried away with him all who saw them or only heard of them" (2003:162). Fo's title, *Lu santo jullàre Françesco*, signals his intention to present Francis as a *jullàre* (an archaic form of *giullare*). He does well to bring our attention to Francis' penchant for communicating via performance, which, as we will see, was in the register of the *giullari*. However, Fo's re-presentation of history is an intrinsic part of his performance framing, and his re-presentation of Francis is based on *his* definition of the *giullare* as a carnivalesque figure, central to his theatre. For the purpose of this study, historical references will be cited for primarily two reasons. First, a general knowledge of the historical background will help to comprehend the crux of Fo's re-presentation of the *giullare*. Second, history will assist in deciphering the complex and enigmatic Saint Francis of Assisi, the central figure of this chapter, who associated himself with the medieval *giulleria*. Contextualizing Francis within the frames of the historical *giullare* and Fo's *giullare* is essential to this analysis of *The Holy Jester Francis*.

Fo began to define the medieval *giullare* in Mistero *buffo*, with the key sketch "The Birth of the *Giullare*." In this sketch Christ appears to a peasant who is about to commit suicide, after suffering unspeakable atrocities at the hands of a nobleman. He miraculously gives the peasant the gift of eloquence, transforms him into a *giullare*, and commands him to travel throughout the land and awaken people to their plight: "You must crush these feudal lords and the clergy and all those who surround them: notaries, attorneys, etc. Not for your own good or for your land, but for all those who have no land, who have nothing and can only suffer, without dignity" (1977b:80).

On more than one occasion Fo asserted that the *giullari* originated from the lower classes, and while many were persecuted for their social criticism, others were taken in by the nobility, in a process that kept them in line and neutralized their satiric bite. "Of course, you had some *giullari* who sold their dignity while betraying their social class . . ." (1974b:24). Chiara Valentini explains how Fo's *giullari* were born of the folk and vented the anger of the downtrodden in a grotesque register.

> And it was for this reason, Fo maintains, the *giullari* were harshly persecuted, and in the Middle Ages many were often flayed or had their tongues cut out. And, with a process that was more subtle . . . their mode of expression was at a certain point absorbed and perverted by the dominant classes. The piazza *giullare* became the court *giullare*, and his clowneries were no longer an instrument of communication with the folk, but served to entertain courtiers and to flatter the sovereign. (1997:124-25)

Fo's simplistic dichotomy of folk versus court *giullari* has led to much debate. Michele Straniero quotes the passage above from Valentini and responds that according to Fo, the *giullare* suffered degradation and integration by the dominant caste or class—integration, which is presented as an exemplary moment of a religious-existential drama, with the interaction of opposing forces: the forces of Good (the folk and the popular *giullare*) and the forces of Evil (the nobility and the court *giullare*). Fo proposes to rectify this with a sort of *redemption* of the "desecrated" figure, who was subdued, deprived of his tongue and of his charismatic and liberating power. . . . (1978:17-18 emphasis in the original)

Separating the *giulleria* into well-delineated, lower and upper class categories is problematic, and Straniero presents some evidence to discredit any simplistic divisions. In fact, the *giullare* remains a complex and diverse figure, whose activities straddled seemingly opposing worlds, including: popular and court; oral and literary; sacred and profane.[3] Many of the songs and stories of the *giulleria* extolled the mystique of noble birth, of courtliness, and of chivalry. Another consideration is the harsh reality of homeless, itinerant performers trying to scrape a living and feed their families. One must logically conclude that an invitation to perform for wealthier patrons, more often than not, would be most welcomed.

Fo's re-presentation of the itinerant medieval performer has become an important part of his carnival frame and indexical code. He portrays the *giullare* essentially as a disseminator of Marxist-Gramscian messages about the exploitation of the masses by the wealthy elite. The accuracy of Fo's portrayal of the *giullare* has less to do with the actual itinerant performer, consciously "upholding the dignity of the downtrodden," and more to do with the *liminoid* icon, akin to the Lord of Misrule, the Jolly Joker, and the Shakespearean fool.[4] This icon embodies carnivalesque defiance of official culture and authority, with its lampooning and satire of authority figures, and license to speak the truth, as long as it is masked in *liminoid* madness.

Fo portrays the despicable court *giullare* as a traitor to his social class, who was willing to limit his satire, in order to let the nobles who were paying him appear to be liberal-minded and open to criticism. His vision of the court *giullare* stands as an emblem of flaccid, contemporary political satire. This is the basis upon which he made his oft quoted statement about ending his role as "the *giullare* of the bourgeoisie," in 1969, when he intended to break away from traditional theatre venues and bring his performances directly to the people (Mitchell 1999:87-88). According to Fo, today's so-called political satire is so toothless that politicians revel in it as a way of showing their human side, sometimes even appearing on television comedy shows that parody them. When I asked him about this in an interview, he responded emphatically, pointing to some of Italy's most important old-guard politicians: "But this is really a boot-licking, a tribute to their quirks and their good-nature. Andreotti was flattered because he came off as a crafty old devil, with clever quips, a cynic who could care less. Craxi was a kindly old chap, and so on" (1993).

Fo's dichotomy of folk versus official culture may be more relevant when applied to the opposition of the carnivalesque aspects of the *giulleria* in the face of Church authority. During the Middle Ages, the Catholic Church was a powerful institution. With its higher clergy drawn from the upper classes, it imposed official culture, even brutally, whenever it saw fit to do so. As we have seen, the *giullare* was marginalized, even demonized, by the Church, which relegated him to no more than an embodiment of "paganism," i.e. of the pre-Christian, European cultural substratum. The carnival and carnivalesque elements of this culture were particularly troublesome to the Church's sense of divine authority.

The *Giullari* and the Mendicant Orders

The relationship between Church and *giullari* changed drastically in the 1200s. This was a result of the founding of the two large orders of mendicant monks, the Franciscans and the Dominicans, both established in the beginning of the century. The Church was moving into public space, formerly the province of the *giullari*, and competing with them for the attention of audiences. In his *Manual for Preaching*, Humbert of Romans (c.1200-77), fifth Master General of the Dominican order, tells his monks to go where the *giullari* go, "to preach in the streets, in the cities, in the great avenues of communication, in the fairs and markets, at tournaments, at funerals, at weddings, at banquets, at parties." Since the *giullari* were adept at gathering crowds and holding their attention, the monks realized that to do likewise, in order to preach and to collect alms, they had something to learn from these performers. Humbert reminds his monks that by preaching they were engaged in a type of performance and advises them to make their words sweet like the songs of the *giullari*. Their sermons must please God, with the same joy the *giullari* create with their songs in the courts of the powerful. However, the Dominican preachers must take care not to emulate the *giullari*'s histrionics or create an atmosphere of gaiety. "The preacher must substitute the *giullari*'s mime and gestures with the composure of his being . . ." (Casagrande and Vecchio 1978:240-41).

The Dominican order was originally established to fight heresy, to promote the Crusades, to uphold the policies of the Roman Church, as well as to preach the Gospel. Throughout European history, they were active in the various Inquisitions. Unlike the early Franciscans, they did not adhere to strict poverty, nor did they live amongst the downtrodden or share the vagabond life of the *giullari*. They preached among the people, but then returned to their monasteries, often situated near urban areas. Although the Dominicans realized that in order to be successful they had to learn from the *giullari*, they did not view them as fellow performers or traveling companions. They were competition, even adversaries. The Dominicans felt it necessary to appropriate their space, and the best case scenario, it seems, would have been for them to simply go away. "For the *giullare* who does not yield the stage to the preacher, like a heretic who insists in his errors, there is no alternative except holy war" (Casagrande and Vecchio 1978:241-43).

In contrast to that of the Dominicans, the Franciscan order developed spontaneously, as more and more people left behind their earthly possessions in order to follow the charismatic Francis. Even women were allowed to join the community which developed around Francis' disciple Clair. They purposely interacted with common folk and did not simply preach and retreat to monasteries. They accepted food and shelter, not money, and were required to work for it. They also helped the sick, in particular those stricken with leprosy who were ostracized and shunned. As we focus on the figure of Francis below, we will take a close look at his direct connection to the *giulleria* and his penchant for performance, for which he is known as *joculator domini* (*giullare* of God). In contrast to the Dominicans' stern approach regarding heretics there was Francis' all-inclusive love for human beings and creatures of God. All of this made for a very different relationship between the Franciscans and the *giullari*.

The English scientist and Franciscan monk, Roger Bacon (1214-93), wrote advice for Franciscan preachers in his *Opus Tertium*. Bacon describes preaching as a theatrical performance that should stir emotions in the spectators. He discusses the use of exempla as an instrument of persuasion, as well as the use of poetry and music. And very distinct from the Dominicans' disdain of the *giullari*'s body language, he defines the body as the greatest instrument. "The expressions of the face, tears, laughter, fear, movements of the whole body . . ." (Casagrande and Vecchio 1978:245). An accomplished scholar, Bacon refers back to the writings of Aristotle and other philosophers, poets, and orators throughout his treatise. But when it comes to gestural and body language, he has only the biographies of Francis to guide him. This aspect of the Saint will be taken up shortly.

Francis had never intended to establish a monastic order. During his short lifetime, he witnessed his original little band of followers grow to a point that was out of his control. The situation required that an official order be founded. Francis had always delivered his message directly to his brothers, not by writing but through exempla, and he was ill-equipped to compose a rule and organize such a large institution. "His Rule was in no sense a set of ethical or legal prescriptions and prohibitions; rather, it was a concrete model for what he considered should be the total '*vita fratum minorum*' [life of a brother minor]" (Turner 1995:143).[5] For example, in the Rule of 1221, he advises his brothers to rejoice when in the company of the downtrodden, the sick, and the indigent. Several years before his death, Francis relinquished control of the order, content to remain in hermitage with a small group of brothers. Within a few decades after his death, the order spread and grew throughout Europe. In the centuries to follow, the order divided into two branches: the Spirituals, who wanted to maintain the rigors of Francis' ideals, including the strict vow of poverty; and the Conventuals, who modified the original intentions of the Saint. Over time the Conventuals predominated and the Spirituals were dissolved. "The influence of successive popes was naturally enough directed towards making the Franciscans, like the rival order of Dominicans, a fitting instrument of policy, both spiritual and political" (Lambert 1961:70).

Giullare, Mystic, and Liminar

During the thirteenth century, in the cities of northern and central Italy, the new merchant class was beginning to compete and share power with the traditional feudal aristocracy. Although the Holy Roman Emperor had issued decrees in an attempt to keep the power within the noble families, there were nevertheless ways in which the members of the upper levels of the merchant class could be co-opted (such as by marriage) into the aristocracy. Young men in this position often acquired horses and armor, and trained for knightly combat, with the hopes of being admitted into the ranks of the nobility. The son of a wealthy cloth merchant, Francis was in this position and, equipped with horses and armor, he aspired to become a knight (Cardini 1989:51-58). What is more, he was infatuated with the romance of chivalry and enamored of the chivalric tradition. He was familiar with tales of knights and ladies and sang songs of chivalric deeds, such as the *chansons de geste*. These were the songs of the troubadours, which were widely popular at the time. The troubadours were originally literate, court *giullari* from southern France, and their songs became an important part of the European *giulleria*. Francis sang these songs in the original Provençal, in which he was fluent. Francis' given name was Giovanni, and *Francesco*, his nickname, affiliated him somehow with France, though it is not altogether clear why. One theory is that his mother may have been of French origin. Another explanation is that his father was in France on business when Francis was born.

Or perhaps it was simply because of his love for the troubadour tradition.

As a young man, Francis belonged to an association of other youths in Assisi who aspired to knighthood. These young men were wont to give parties, and it seems Francis often hosted these celebrations (using, we can safely assume, his father's money). The tradition was that the member who paid for the party would be *rex* (king) of the festivities, and given to hold a symbolic rod, suggesting the scepter of a fool or jester. Cardini explains, "the custom of proclaiming someone *rex* during a party is well known to sociologists. We are in the ambit . . . of *saturnalicius rex* [king of the Saturnalia], which in the Middle Ages bordered on the customs of the *giullaria*." Within the liminality of the celebrations, the *rex* was essentially a *liminoid* Lord of Misrule. Discussing Francis' association with the *giulleria*, Franco Cardini writes, "it is certain he possessed outstanding *giullaresque* talents. And he combined these with extravagant ways, typical of that mode of expression, such as the custom of adorning oneself in *centunculus* of the mime and *giullare* of his time." *Centunculus* was a motley garment made of many small pieces, combining very expensive cloth together with poor rags.[6] (He certainly would have had access to expensive cloth from his father's business.) Considering various aspects of young Francis' extravagant behavior, including his motley dress, we can conclude,

> he behaved like a fool, and his continuous merriment and his outbursts of joy confirm this. But the fool has a precise standing in the context of the medieval city as well as in chivalric culture: he for whom all is permissible, the marginalized person who is accepted in the courts of princes . . . The *giullari*, in the manner in which they dress and express themselves, are fools. . . . (Cardini 1989:58, 60-61)

Francis' conviction to lead an ascetic life followed a period of transition and indecision. The moment that marks the definitive break with his former existence is the public confrontation with his father, mediated by the local Bishop. Francis removes his clothing and hands it back to his father, proclaiming that his only father, from that point on, will be God. These actions establish certain themes that will define his saintly life. Perhaps as a reaction to his previous life of wealth and privilege, he adheres to a strict rule of absolute poverty that went beyond any monastic rule of that time. With reference to Christ's words, "Render therefore unto Caesar the things which are Caesar's" (Mat 21:22), he refuses to deal with money. And having stripped himself publically in a symbolic gesture, nakedness continued to be "the master symbol of emancipation from structural and economic bondage, as from the constraints set upon him by his earthly father, the wealthy merchant of Assisi" (Turner 1995:146).

The other aspect of his former life, which continued after his *conversio*, was his association with the *giulleria*. His *giullaresque* activities as an enlightened saint continued to be in the chivalric register, using the knight's code of honor as a metaphor for leading the Christian life. His courtly lady, whom he would serve as a faithful knight, was Lady Poverty and his conquest was the conquest of himself. "He created a code of ethics, using as a model the heroic virtues of knights and paladins" (Frugoni 1995:37). Cardini discusses an early episode, about two years after his *conversio*, in which Francis is beaten up by bandits. When they first encounter him and demand to know who he is (already disappointed by the fact that there is obviously nothing to steal), Francis declares, "I am the herald of the great King. Does this interest you?" Cardini expounds on Francis' declaration:

> He was certainly a madman [fool], one who had chosen to subscribe to a form of madness that was very close to the rigorously formalized madness of the *giullaresque lazzi*. The word "herald" leaves us no doubt: the herald . . . is the most authoritative amongst the *giullari* present at a tournament. He is the one who is able to recognize the coat of arms of the participating knights and proclaim their merits and acts of valor. (1989:100)

The *giullaresque* register continued to be Francis' vehicle of communication. Amongst the documented episodes of his life, one incident in particular illustrates this point. Francis preached to a group of noblemen in Romagna who were in the midst of a celebration. "Whatever could a cleric have accomplished at a knights' party? But a *giullare*, yes. A *giullare* would have been in his element" (Cardini 1989:167). Francis' first biographer, Tommaso da Celano, captured the essence of Francis' performance-based means of communication with this description: "he spoke with his entire body" (*de toto corpore fecerat linguam*). Da Celano also notes the subtleties of Francis' communicative talents: "He would suggest in a few words what was beyond expression, and using fervent gestures and nods, he would transport his hearers to heavenly things" (Habig 1983:450).

From our modern perspective, some of Francis' performances may appear to be grotesque or farcical. When he celebrated Christmas at the stable at Greccio, where he created a tableau with live actors depicting the birth of Christ in the manger (considered the origin of the crèche tradition), he bleated the word "Bethlehem" like a lamb.[7] Once, after eating meat, he had a brother lead him through the streets by a rope like a criminal, shouting, "Behold the glutton!" Erich Auerbach explains, "But in their time and place such scenes did not produce a farcical effect. Their arrestingness, exaggeration, vividness did not appear shocking, but as a graphic, exemplary revelation of a saintly life, directly illuminating, comprehensible to all, and inspiring all to examine themselves in comparison and to share the experience" (2003:168). It is also important to keep in mind that Francis' histrionic examples, though extraordinary, were part of a tradition of *giullaresque* preachers. We have evidence of other such preachers, Giovanni Bono for example, who were active during Francis' time (Cardini 1989:159-60).

It is easy to be led astray, however, by Francis' *giullaresque* register and his emphasis on performance. He was *joculator domini*, but this was the means by which he delivered his message, not the message itself. What defined Saint Francis more than anything else was his complete dedication to the Gospel, in its pure form, free of theological glossing. As Da Celano states, "Francis' highest intention, his chief desire, his uppermost purpose was to observe the holy Gospel in all things and through all things and, with perfect vigilance, with all zeal, with all the longing of his mind and all the fervor of his heart, 'to follow the teaching and the footsteps of our Lord Jesus Christ'" (Habig 1983:299, the last phrase is from John 2:18). His mystical absorption with the suffering Christ drove him to alleviate the suffering of others, while paying little attention to his own (it is also the basis for the legend of his stigmata). The life he led earned him the epithet of *imitator christi* (imitator of Christ). And if joy was part of his message and laughter an expression of his joy, it was no longer the carnivalesque laughter of the *saturnalicius rex*. His joy was generated by a mystical ecstasy, rather than satirical sting.[8] In discussing Francis' journey to Islam and his meeting with Sultan al-Kamil, Cardini notes why it is very plausible, as Da Celano's version suggests, that the sultan would have treated him with great hospitality: ". . . he was defenseless and dirty and ragged enough to appear as a madman, and Islam shared traditional Christendom's respect for fools. But Francis' [appearance and demeanor] was likewise that of an ascetic, a sage: a sufi . . . which he certainly was in the literal sense of the word" (1989:197).[9] In the Islamic world, sufi denotes an ascetic in the tradition of ecstatic mysticism.

If the enlightened Francis did not share carnivalesque satire with the *giullare*, he nevertheless shared a state of marginalization with regard to the social structure. His extreme social liminality falls into Turner's definition of a *liminar*,

> as persons undergoing ritualized transitions may be termed—of doing without property, structural status, privileges, material pleasures of various kinds, often even clothing. Francis who conceived of his friars as liminars in a life that was merely a passage to the unchanging state of heaven, laid great emphasis on the implications of being "without" or "not having." (1995:144)

In *The Ritual Process*, Turner examines states of liminality that suggest "permanent transition," marked by weakness, passivity, and inferiority. He notes how these "powers of the weak" are often threatening to those "concerned with the maintenance of structure" (1995:109).

Francis' register of spirituality was in contradiction to the Church's solemnity and austerity. His means of communicating through performance and histrionics were closer to the spirit of popular spectacle of the time and stood in sharp contrast to the somber notions of official holiness, with its "intolerant one-sided tone of seriousness" (Bakhtin 1984:73). The renowned medievalist

Umberto Eco makes this clear in his historical novel *The Name of the Rose*. Here he confronts Franciscan joy with official austerity, as the villain Jorge, a Benedictine monk, lashes out at William of Baskerville, a Franciscan. Jorge directs particular invective at Francis' *giullaresque* nature: "You are worse than the Devil, Minorite," Jorge said. "You are a clown [tr. *giullare*], like the saint who gave birth to you all. You are like your Francis, who *de toto corpore fecerat linguam*, who preached sermons giving a performance like a mountebank's . . ." (1983:477-78). Francis, who by his very nature was a *liminar*, was in some ways subversive with respect to Church authority. To begin with, he did not choose to simply join one of the established monastic orders and be contained within its structure. His penchant for performance and his expression of joy was threatening to the Church's solemnity and austerity. But despite all of this, he never outwardly defied authority. The Minorites' golden rule was to "be humble and tolerate everything."

Fo's Francis

In *Elizabeth* Fo's Shakespeare was reminiscent of Fo: a playwright of the working-class. In the two plays where he presents Ruzzante, the Paduan playwright "is to some extent remade in Fo's own image and likeness" (Farrell 2000b:99). As one might expect, a conspicuous aspect of Fo's historical re-presentation of Francis contextualizes him in the carnival frame and portrays him as a Fo-*giullare*, which he defined in *Mistero buffo*. It should be clear however that historically Fo's folk-versus-court dichotomy is not applicable to Francis, who shared the *giullare*'s status as fool, but embraced the idealism of courtliness and chivalry as part of his communicative code.

Francis was on Fo's mind years before he produced *The Holy Jester*. When I interviewed him, a discussion on laughter segued to his thoughts on Saint Francis:

> People need to laugh like they need to make love, to eat, to breathe. A people that does not laugh is criminal. . . . The great revolution of Saint Francis was precisely to laugh, to smile, to be

ironic, to play down one's own importance and understand that what matters are the simple, everyday things in life. It wasn't the Pope. It was water, the sun, the earth, the air, fire, the sea, these were the important things in life. Not catechisms. In fact, he is one of the few [saints] who did not write a catechism. Saint Francis' rule was a rule of how to live in relation to others. He did not simply say, "Don't kill," but he said, "If your enemy loses his sword, pick it up and hand it back to him." He also said, "in the worst criminal you will find something good. Try to guide him."[10] He was precisely one who would not say that Muslims are infidels who have to be destroyed. He went to the Muslims. He went to speak with them, and the Caliph, the leader of the Muslims, understood this was an extraordinary person. (1993)

Even at this stage, his vision of Francis was in the Fo-*giullare* register: "Why was Francis called 'the *giullare* of God'? Not because he made God laugh, but 'of God' in the sense that he was sent 'by God.' The *giullare* sent by God. To do what? To mock, to tease, to pull your leg, to sing, to dance, to enjoy, to live, and to smile. And then he was full of *lazzi* . . ." (1993).

In the prologue to *The Holy Jester*, Fo explains he used to believe the epithet "*giullare* of God" was perhaps added a century or more after Francis' death (1999a:3). In the video performance he says, "This is the great discovery, as far as I am concerned. I discovered in the texts, the accounts, and above all, in the chronicles, a true *giullare*" (1999b). He drives this home by repeating "Francis was a *giullare*" several times. In both the text and the video he emphasizes Chiara Frugoni's book, where he learned that Francis had proclaimed himself a *giullare*. He adds his commentary concerning his folk-versus-court dichotomy: "To saddle yourself with the status of a satirical buffoon in the beginning of the thirteenth century was a very dangerous provocation of suicidal madness. The *giullari* were loved by the common folk, but hated and persecuted by the powerful, who would put these clowns in the pillory at every chance" (1999a:3-4). The episode Frugoni refers to is the same as the one cited above, where Francis declares, "I am the herald of the great king!" which Frugoni, like Cardini, links to the chivalric tradition (1995:30).

It is evident Fo is claiming historical *auctoritas* while simultaneously suggesting his own re-presentation. Here, unlike *Mistero buffo*, the ruse is made clear:

> Of the text I'm about to perform there is no written document. I have taken the liberty with great recklessness to reconstruct it, using accounts and chronicles of the time. I am not going to verify it, you'll have to trust me! And when—and I'm sure—in the near future the original text will resurface, as this has happened in past centuries with other writings on Francis, you can exclaim: "I already knew it!" (1999a:6)

By deciding to portray Saint Francis of Assisi in his epic-theatre style, whereby he never gets fully into character and continues to be himself, Fo takes on a delicate balancing act. Whereas he has established himself concretely as an unrepentant critic of official culture, including its manipulation of religion, the historical figure he represents was unequivocally in diametric opposition. As Frugoni explains, "Francis does not offer a political response to the social injustices or the problems of the world. He has no plans to bring about effective and concrete changes. He does not contemplate struggle and rebellion" (1995:24). Fo had to keep his portrayal within some semblance of reasonable bounds, with regards to the Minorite's liminal qualities, or else risk presenting a parody of the Saint. While he does present a Francis who is "full of irony" (1999b) and who incites people to oppose the power structure, one obvious modification was made, specifically with regard to Fo's usual criticism of religion.

An important theme Fo established in *Mistero buffo* is the dichotomy of the tyrannical God the Father versus the loving son Jesus. The former became an instrument of official culture, used as a weapon of cosmic terror to keep people in line, while the latter was closer to the heart and sensibilities of folk religion. In the prologue to the key sketch "The Massacre of the Innocents" Fo explains, "That is why God the Father is so hated, because he represents those in power. It is He who bestows crowns and privileges; while Jesus Christ is loved, for it is He who comes to earth to try and give back the spring and above all dignity" (1977b:28-29). This is one of Fo's most important religious themes. The portrayal of the callous, authoritative paternalistic God was present in early stories of *Poer nano*, such as "Cain and Abel," and appears in various forms throughout his *giullarate*. Within this context, Fo's characters are wont to openly express fervent hostilities towards God. In the "Massacre of the Innocents," a grieving mother vents her anger: "Terrible, pitiless God! . . . This killing is your doing! It was you who wanted this sacrifice in order to allow your son to descend. One thousand children butchered for the sake of one of yours. A river of blood for one little cup" (1977b:36). Again in *Johan Padan*, after the Indios hear how Christ died on the cross: "Cruel and evil God! . . . When your son yelled, 'Father help me,' why did you pretend like nothing was happening, so you could stay up there playing the guitar with the angels? You left him to croak like a dog!" (1992e:91). Often Fo presents an angel as God's envoy, as mentioned in the previous chapter, who by proxy becomes the target of folk anger.[11]

Fo's Francis, as *imitator christi*, is informed by Fo's Jesus, whom he conceptualizes within folk culture. This Jesus, who in "The Birth of the *Giullare*" transforms the abused and powerless peasant into a satirical revolutionary, represents a continuation of Dionysus-Bacchus (1977b:53-54). This is suggested in "The Wedding at Cana," which is a scene inserted within *The Holy Jester*. Here Fo's Jesus stands on the table and pours wine. But unlike in his other *giullarate*, hostility towards God the Father is drastically toned down. In the prologue Fo explains that Francis' use of poetry and song was his means to express "the theme of joyous love that we owe our Creator" (1999a:4). There is criticism towards official religion, but it is directed primarily at the Church as an institution and in particular towards the office of the papacy. The one jab at the paternalistic God is taken indirectly, by means of alluding to the indexical frame.

The Structure of *The Holy Jester*

The five episodes that comprise the main body of *The Holy Jester* are 1) "Francis' Harangue in Bologna"; 2) "The Expulsion of the Nobility and the Shaking of the Forty Toppled Towers"; 3) "The Holy Jester and the Wolf of Gubbio"; 4) "Saint Francis Goes to the Pope in Rome"; and 5) "Saint Francis Goes Off to Die." Three additional tales (not on the accompanying video) are included in the text under "Other Stories": "The Battle Against the Perugians," "Saint Francis and the Chicken," "Francis and the Sultan of Zime al Beny." In the published text, the five primary episodes are arranged with facing pages, Italian and archaic dialect,[12] while the "Other Stories" are only in dialect. In performance, Fo stands before a backdrop he painted with images representing key moments of the play. A sketch of the backdrop appears as a frontispiece to this volume.

Typically in his *giullarate* (most of which are comprised of separate sketches), besides the main prologue delivered before the performance, each sketch is introduced by its own mini-prologue. *The Holy Jester* has an extended prologue, as well as short prologues to the first two sketches. Fo then makes a transition between the second episode, "The Expulsion of the Nobility," and the third, "The Wolf of Gubbio," with a connecting tale. This transition tale is accompanied by a codeswitch of great significance in the *giullarata* context. Whereas Fo uses standard Italian for his informative prologue, he executes the performance proper in a dialect-based language. The connecting tale, in this case, is delivered in Italian, before he announces, "at this point begins the *giullarata* of the wolf" (1999a:37). It therefore functions simultaneously as part of the narrative and as an introduction, presenting the events leading first to Francis' enlightenment and then to the tale of the wolf. The transitions from the third episode, "The Wolf of Gubbio," to the fourth, "Saint Francis Goes to the Pope in Rome," and then from the fourth to the fifth, "Saint Francis Goes Off to Die," are similar in that each consists of a brief statement explaining that "the following episode needs no introduction" (59, 89).

Francis' Harangue in Bologna

In this first sketch we find a mature, enlightened Francis. The sketches of *The Holy Jester* are presented out of chronological order, since the following episode flashes back to a younger, pre-*conversio* Francis. There are two explanations for this structure, and it may be that both contributed to the decision to lead off with this scene. The first is that the language of the Umbrian Francis' harangue is Neapolitan (i.e. colored with Neapolitan cadence and intonation). In consequence, one possibility is that this sketch may have come first in order to dispense with the Neapolitan as soon as possible and allow the rest of the performance to flow in Fo's usual *giullarata* language. The other reason may be that this sketch defines Francis by contextualizing him squarely within Fo's *giullare*. It sets the tone for the rest of the performance, with cutting sarcasm and slapstick gags.

In the prologue, Fo explains that the reason for having Francis speak in Neapolitan will become obvious (though there may be an added touch of unwarranted mystique). He then has the saint pretend that he expected to be in Naples and thus prepared his talk accordingly. Perhaps what is suggested here is a facetious disclaimer, like Plautus setting his plays in Greece. But Francis goes on to acknowledge his mistake and addresses the people of Bologna directly. In any event, this is very effective in presenting Francis as a medieval fool: "You're not Neapolitans? (*Brief pause*) And where are you from? From Bologna?! (*Brief pause*) All of you?" (8).

The basis for the "harangue" is an account by Tommaso da Spalato, who in 1222, while a student at Bologna, heard Francis deliver a sermon on "angels, men, and demons." He notes how Francis used a colloquial, more secular style of speaking (*modus concionandi*) instead of the preaching style that was typical of the clergy (*modus praedicandi*) (Habig 1983:1601-02). The contrast between Francis' rhetoric and Fo's is striking. "In the saint's plan—another point to be underscored—positive example is the only means to persuade someone to change and reform. [This is accomplished] by means of example more so than of words, which, however, should never sound an attack or make an accusation, but only fraternal exhortation" (Frugoni 1995:53). In "Francis' Harangue," by facetiously exalting the glory of war, Fo has Francis criticizing the bellicose nature of the Bolognese and all of the conflicts, both internal and external, in which they were involved. The blatant contrast between the subversive clown and the humble saint is one of register. Fo pretends to exalt war by means of sarcastic praise, very much in an ironic register, typical of Fo and not of Francis. There is also an anachronistic tone, which makes the humor immediate to the contemporary audience: "Great to have an enemy, an enemy to slaughter!" (12); "It was a triumphant massacre!" (14); "Ah! What a holy massacre! Wonderful! Well done!" (14). There is also grotesque slapstick, as Fo describes men returning from war without limbs. One veteran, congratulated for his bravery, must shake hands using his foot. Delivering one of his typical invectives, complete with zany gags, Fo projects himself into the character of the most popular saint of Christendom.

Fo/Francis conveys the effect of his tirade by the reaction of his imaginary audience. "Hey you women, but why are you crying? What's the matter? I know you. You're the mother of that fellow who was killed in the war. And you? Your father was killed" (16). This segues into a socio-political message, delivered with the same irony: "Oh God! This is a disaster! I hear you don't want to listen to the holy speeches of the magistrates. You're beginning to think for yourselves, to reason with your own brains, your own heads! This is a very grave danger" (18). Fo's genius here is demonstrated in his ability to play several registers at once. He changes tone and dwells on the word "peace": "Peace. Ah, what a beautiful word: peeaace!" This register shift, from ironic sarcasm to a genuine longing for peace, leads into a folk song that rejoices in the everyday events of peasant life: the sunrise, rain, tilling the soil, children growing, a wedding celebration. Here Fo makes use of his indexical code to inform Francis with the qualities of his mirthful Dionysian Jesus. In "The Wedding at Cana" in *Mistero buffo*, Jesus stands on the table, pouring wine for the guests: "Drink up people, be merry, get drunk, don't wait for later, have fun!" (1977b:66). Likewise Francis sings, "Drink, drink, to your health, I'm getting drunk, be happy, be happy!" (20). Fo returns to the "The Wedding at Cana" again later in the play.

Tommaso da Spalato relates that in the sermon in Bologna, Francis "spoke of the duty of putting an end to hatreds and of arranging a new treaty of peace" (Habig 1983:1601). By contrast Fo's Marxist jester incites people to actively bring about social change: "In a day or two, you'll go to the town hall and ask the magistrate to sign a peace treaty with all your enemies, and even to make peace with all the lords fighting here in Bologna" (18). While da Spalato explains that "God conferred so much power in his words that they brought back peace in many a seignorial family torn apart until then by old, cruel, and furious hatreds" (1601-02), in Fo's version, three days following Francis' harangue, "the people did in fact go to protest at the town hall and all the city officials were compelled to meet and sign a peace treaty, the 'Concilium Pacis.' This document still exists in Bologna" (22).

The Backdrop and The Expulsion of the Nobility

As was mentioned above, Fo performs *The Holy Jester* while standing before a painted backdrop. Being an accomplished artist, he often begins a play by drawing and/or painting a type of storyboard, representing key moments. On more than one occasion, instead of a written text, he has used the images directly as a mnemonic device. The images present a series of formulaic units, based on key moments in the story. For *Johan Padan* Fo kept a book with the iconography on a lectern and referred to it during the performance. He also demonstrated this technique in his acceptance speech for the Nobel Prize. Instead of a scripted text, he handed out twenty-five pages of brightly colored drawings. The audience turned the pages along with him, as he extemporized his talk based on the images.[13]

In the prologue to "The Expulsion of the Nobility and the Forty Toppled Towers," Fo refers to the backdrop behind him. He explains he had painted the original images and that a group of artists copied them to the backdrop. Most of the images of Francis are relatively straightforward with regard to conventional iconography of the saint in medieval art (with the obvious exception of being in Fo's distinctive style). He indicates that, besides "the salient events" he will perform, there is "a band of flying witches and other mythical images of Umbrian folklore, that originate with the Etruscans and the Greeks" (22). In addition, there are images of voluptuous naked women, typical of Fo's paintings. In the main prologue he mentions that Francis' *giullaresque* register included sexuality. In fact the song cited in the preceding episode includes, "The youngest daughter makes love in the cellar/ . . . / the daughter is in love and becomes pregnant / we must rush a wedding" (20).[14] The backdrop is an artistic touch of genius, for it visually takes the story of Saint Francis beyond the conventions of hagiographic representation. With figures from pre-Christian paganism along with blatant images of sexuality, it functions to keep the performance within his carnival frame.

The episode of "The Expulsion" is based on a historical event which took place in 1198, when Francis would have been about sixteen or seventeen years old. The *boni homines*, the privileged nobles of Assisi, were attacked and expelled by the *homines populi*, the other social classes of the city, including the lower classes together with the new mercantile class. The nobles' fortified structures within the city, including their towers, were then razed. We are not sure if Francis participated in this rebellion. We know he participated several years later in a battle against the *boni homines* and their allies from Perugia. Francis was captured and spent one year in prison. After his return to Assisi, it took about another year to recover from illness and depression. In the meantime, the *boni homines* returned and reestablished themselves.

Fo begins re-presenting the expulsion by making two changes to the historical accounts. First, he claims Francis did participate in the revolt, but that this fact is often left out of the chronicles and hagiography. Once again, he suggests to the audience that the reason will become clear to them. The second aspect of his historical re-presentation is his claim that "Francis literally betrays the social class to which he belonged" (23). As was stated above, the members of the mercantile class were part of the *homines populi*. Fo thus depicts the young Francis as a revolutionary. He explains how the nobles tried to impose their political will while refusing to pay taxes. He then connects past and present with a touch of sarcasm:

"a completely local phenomenon, tied exclusively to the Middle Ages!" (23).

The sketch opens with the crowds of Assisi attaching ropes to the towers and pulling them down. Slowed down and restricted in his movements from age and a stroke, Fo is nonetheless still able to invoke a scene of multitudes with his extraordinary *giullaresque* talents. He simultaneously acts, narrates, and even inserts a metanarrational break: "Congratulations! You even understand expressions in pure Bergamasque!" referring to his Lombard-based performance language (26). The sturdiest tower requires some extra effort, and Francis is among the young men who climb up to attach the ropes to the belfry. There is an accident and Francis is sent swinging through the air by a rope, smacking into walls and clanking into the bells. (The idea of swinging off a tower by a rope is found in Fo's early work, also in a medieval setting, *The True Story of Piero D'Angera*.) The effect is cartoonlike, as the episode is filled with onomatopoeic sounds (especially of the bells). Slapstick gags, and jokes, abound as poor Francis flies helplessly through the air, is bruised and battered, and then manages to fall down a long flight of stairs. He is carried home, and his mother screams, thinking he is dead. "Mother, don't yell. I have twelve bells clanking in my head!" They bring him down to convalesce in the wine cellar. "Silence! Nobody breathe!" (30).

After seven days he reemerges, to the jokes and teasing of his pals. Although this episode is in a light and zany register, the jokes and comments reveal its function in the play. When his friends ask him to ring matins, and he answers by simulating the sounds of a bell, Fo the narrator comments, "Because Francis was a man of spirit [wit], as well as spiritual" (32). He then explains that after he became a saint, his friends attributed his enlightenment to the accident: "After that terrific ringing he was never the same. He'd go around, looking up, as if enchanted . . . he would point to the moon, and to the moon he'd say 'Hello Sister!' And then to the stars 'Little Sisters,' to the sun 'Brother,' to the earth 'Mother Earth.' One big family! Then he'd talk with animals, with the birds, and he'd bless them!" (32). Fo is aware that mystical ecstasy is the primary difference that separates his Holy Jester from the historical one. Here he blatantly subverts any notion of mysticism and spirituality and places Francis squarely within the definition of his *giullare*.

The Holy Jester and the Wolf of Gubbio

The famous tale of how Francis pacified the wolf of Gubbio is found in the most widely read collection of stories about the saint, known as *The Little Flowers of Saint Francis*, written by a Franciscan monk about a century after the saint's death. Some of the stories from the *Little Flowers* are well known in the Italian oral tradition, especially among older generations. The tale of the wolf of Gubbio is part of the greater motif of the saint's mystical relationship with animals, both domestic and wild. This motif is found in various sources on Saint Francis, as well as in other mystical tradition around the world.

Fo's "Wolf of Gubbio," wherein human and animals converse, is reminiscent of "Tale of the Tiger." The wolf's speech is a combination of words and feral sounds, as the stage directions read, "He answers emitting guttural, roaring sounds" (40). As we saw in the last chapter, Fo uses the wolf as an allegory for humans' bestial nature. To the wolf's explanation that his behavior is natural to a wolf, Francis continues the animal/human allegory and counters that this is a weak excuse: "And those who don't have this natural inclination? The unfortunate and the wretched, who must get used to beatings and kicks in the ass . . ." (42). At this point in the performance, the audience expresses its appreciation of the allegory by applauding, forcing Fo to pause. This is a clear example of the effectiveness of his indexical frame, where the theme of the abuse of power by exploiters at the expense of the exploited is prominent. Though the message and the register are Fo's, his use of animals as allegory is very much in line with Francis': "The greediness of the robin, the violence of the sow, are not in reality evils in and of themselves, but stand rather as negative models, as the forms of evil that man may commit" (Cardini 1989:238).

When Francis travels to get building stones for a church he is restoring, one of the quarrymen explains he must ask permission from the Celestine monks, who had asked the pope for rights to the quarry. He gave it to them, on oral agreement, for two months. Then the pope died and the monks continue to control the quarry. Here he has Francis direct a jab at the office of the papacy: "Why, because the pope is dead?! Goshdarnit! They even cheat us when they're dead!" (46). After being driven away by the Celestines, followed by an adventure with a band of brigands, which ends in a drunken party, the wolf discusses the primary problem with his conversion to good behavior. It is impossible for him to remain a vegetarian. Francis tells him, "I'll give you some advice, but don't tell anyone or you'll ruin my reputation" (56). He tells the wolf to be a vegetarian as much as he can, but when he can stand it no longer, to kill a young goat or a calf. Occasionally killing a small animal will be acceptable, as long as he does it by "directing attention towards God." The incredulous wolf exclaims, "Attention towards God?" and Francis explains,

> Yes. Do you remember Adam, Eve, Cain and Abel? Abel, for example, in order to be loved by God, what did he do? He'd grab a lamb, he'd bring it to the mountain, and there he'd slaughter it and put it on the fire, and roast it filled with aromatic herbs. The smoke would rise up, God who was among the clouds would look down. "What a wonderful smell of roast! Whose is it?"
>
> "It is I, my Lord, Abel. This is dedicated to you."
>
> "Oh, what a lovely gift! How I like this smell! Thank you Abel, I love you!"
>
> And you wolf, do the same! Kill a calf, a little one, bring it to a hill, burn it a little with a bit of herbs. The smoke will rise and God will peek out of the clouds. "Oooh! What a sweet aroma! Who sends me this fragrant gift? A wolf?! Oooh! Blessed be my dear beast! Thank you!"
>
> But pay attention. When God turns around, SNAP! You eat the calf! (58)

This is the point where Fo manages to get in his usual parody of the paternalistic God. There are no direct criticisms leveled or hostilities vented. But by way of the indexical frame, he alludes to his established themes criticizing God the Father, and the audience acknowledges the references with a round of applause. Fo is simultaneously alluding to two of his oldest stories, both of which go back to the stories of *Poer nano*: "Cain and Abel" and "The Sacrifice of Isaac."[15] "Cain and Abel" became a sketch in *Mistero buffo*. "Isaac" became a sketch in *The Tale of a Tiger and Other Stories*, and is retold by Johan to the Indios in *Johan Padan*.[16] Thus both tales are a well-established part of his indexical frame.

By alluding to "Cain and Abel," he connects to his theme of a fickle God, who unfairly favors one brother over the other. In both tales God looks down from the clouds, but it is more developed in "Isaac": "You must know that at that time, it was an ancient time, the world was closer to the sky. . . . And every day one could see God looking down upon his creation, with his great beard, with his elbows on a cloud, as if leaning on a windowsill" (1980:165). It is precisely when Fo enacts the paternalistic God looking down from the clouds that the audience applauds, in recognition of this prevalent theme. In the version of "Isaac" in *Johan Padan*, there is the motif of God's appreciation for the smell of cooked meat, but in this case it would have been Isaac's flesh. Finally, by having Francis teach a wild animal to cook meat, Fo inserts a reference to the primordial mythological theme, which he had developed in "Tale of the Tiger." This associates the Old Testament God with the primitive notion of burnt sacrifice, and keeps *The Holy Jester* within the scope of the prehistoric carnival frame.

Saint Francis Goes to the Pope in Rome

"Let's pick up another story of Francis. This episode does not need an introduction, but has a title, 'Saint Francis Goes to the Pope in Rome.'" With this brief introduction, Fo moves to the next episode. Francis is walking along, when several youths approach him and ask if he would give his blessing at a wedding celebration nearby. They accompany him to the party, and he gives his blessing by telling the New Testament story of "The Wedding at Cana." Fo has Francis tell the tale, which was told by a drunk in *Mistero buffo*. The version in *The Holy Jester* includes several humorous variations, for example, Jesus cracks his knuckles, as if he is about to perform a stunt or magic trick. He makes the sign of the cross over the water, of which "no one recognizes the meaning, because Jesus had not spoken a word yet about his demise, nailed to the cross" (64). And the wine is praised in anachronistic terms, parodying wine-tasting jargon: "Rich in flavor, slight residual sugar with a hint of bitterness in the center, a touch of sparkle, a suggestion of salt, a golden year!" The description continues by spiraling into the grotesque, including belching that exits via the nose, and ending with a touch of blasphemy and a play on words: "God, what a wine! Bravo Jesus! You're divine!" (64). Besides using "God" as an exclamatory, the Italian "divino" (divine) is a pun on "di vino" (of wine).

The retelling of "The Wedding at Cana" immediately follows the allusion to his other inverted Bible stories. By repeating the same technique, Fo juxtaposes his positive image of Jesus to his parody of the paternalistic God. While continuing his playful parody of spirituality, he presents Jesus as an integrated member of the folk community, sanctioning its celebration, and, as a continuation of Dionysian culture, exalting wine. Fo's Jesus informs Francis, who is both *imitator christi* as well as a participant in the folk festivities. After telling the story, Francis is approached by a friendly priest, who informs him that by preaching the Gospel without the permission of higher clergy, he and his brothers are at risk of being imprisoned or burnt at the stake. Francis decides to take his brothers and their request directly to the pope.

From various sources we can determine that Francis traveled with his brothers to Rome and met with Pope Innocent III (1160-1216). They requested their mission be sanctioned and that the pope grant them permission to preach the Gospel. Fo's episode is based on an account by Roger of Wendover. According to this account, when Pope Innocent III first met with Francis, seeing him ragged and disheveled and considering his petition to have the strict rule of poverty sanctioned, he said to him, "Go, brother, find some pigs, to whom you could better compare yourselves. Roll with them in the mud, and, having blessed them, propose to them the rule which you have prepared." Francis humbly follows these orders and returns to the pope: "My Lord, I've done as you commanded; now, I pray you, grant my request" (Cardini 1989:120).

In Fo's rendition, the pope realizes that the Franciscans' poverty and humility is closer to the teachings of Christ and holds an uncomfortable mirror to the Church's opulence. Innocent reacts as if Francis is out to make him look bad, "I'm on to you." Then, by explaining to Francis what he believes he is up to, he proceeds to point out his own hypocrisy. In this way, Fo has the pope himself criticize the papacy: "[W]hat right have I to be the representative of God on earth? I have nothing to do with someone who had no possessions or power. I have lands and palaces, an entire kingdom, I'm more than a king!" (80).[17] In Wendover's account, the pope concludes by telling Francis to bring his discourse to "the right people," ordering him to go preach to pigs. Fo extends the carnival imagery and heightens the pitch by adding, "Then kiss them and roll with them, cut capers in pig piss and pig shit" (80), and by having Francis follow the orders to the letter, rolling in the "shitty mud" (82). He further amplifies the grotesque human/animal contact and suggests primordial mythology by having Francis nurse on the tits of a sow. When he returns, covered in and smelling of pig feces, he interrupts an exquisite dinner the pope is enjoying with noble guests. Jubilantly recounting how he cavorted with the pigs, he splatters feces on all the guests, even causing one noblewoman to vomit (82-84). It should be noted that during the medieval carnival, the splattering of feces was one of the many ways of leveling the social order, by defacing certain members of the community.

Innocent III is infuriated, but before he can react and vent his rage on the impudent fool, he is stopped by Francis' friend, Cardinal Colonna, advisor to the pope. Colonna sternly admonishes him for having provoked such a scene with his outrageous instructions, and reminds him that Francis simply followed his orders. He informs the pope that Francis is loved by the people, and if he should be harmed they will have a popular uprising on their hands. Fo uses the cardinal to allude to popular revolution, which would have been extremely out of character for Francis. Colonna convinces the pope to accept Francis, and the pope is obliged to embrace the saint. "Forgive me Francis, I deserve this. I intended to get shit on you, and I ended up getting shit all over myself!" (84). The image of the pope, in his fine attire, embracing the shit-covered *giullare* is perhaps the strongest of Fo's subversions of papal authority, since Boniface VIII was kicked in the behind by Christ in *Mistero buffo*.

In the first biography of the Saint, by Tommaso Da Celano, Francis and his brothers came across a great number of birds. "When . . . Francis saw them, being a man of great fervor and great tenderness towards lower and irrational creatures, left his companions in the road and ran eagerly towards the birds." The birds do not fly away from him and appear to listen to his sermon. They let him walk among them and touch them before he gives them leave to fly away. This is followed by another story whereby Francis is trying to preach to a gathered crowd, but has to compete with the chattering of many swallows in a nearby tree. Francis addresses the birds, asks them to be silent, and, to the astonishment of the crowd, they obey (Habig 1983:277-78). Variations on these tales exist in both in written and oral traditions and are among the most well-known and beloved stories of the saint. It is not surprising Fo includes a version in his play.

After his meeting with the pope, Francis goes to the market and begins to preach to the crowds. Still covered in feces, he is taken for a raving lunatic and stoned. He then leaves the walls of the city, goes out into the fields, and preaches to the birds that have gathered in a tree. As he preaches, other birds, of all colors and sizes, from the fields, forests, mountains, and sea, gather to listen. Reportedly when the historical Francis preached to birds, his primary theme was from the Gospel: "Consider the ravens: for they neither sow nor reap . . . and God feedeth them" (Luke 12:24). He explains to the creatures why they should give thanks to their creator for providing for them and giving them the wondrous ability to fly. Fo takes the opportunity, once again, to contrast human and animal natures. His Francis turns the sermon into a critique of human selfishness, power-struggles, and exploitation.

> Oh blessed birds, free and light, you live without burdens that weigh you down to the earth. No power oppresses you. In contrast we humans find ourselves crushed and loaded like porters with vainglory, avarice, and the gluttony to poses. We are crushed by the folly of gathering possessions while subjugating others in the process, climbing on the heads of others in order to

emerge on top. If we by magic could free ourselves of this burden, stripped of these misguided passions, we would be so light that we could lift ourselves towards the sky. Even the breath of a child would give us flight. (88)

This sermon represents another touch of genius. Fo maintains the flavor of Francis' praise of God's creatures, while he simultaneously tweaks Francis' messages. Francis did preach absolute brotherly love, and he and his Minorites rejected the acquisition of possessions. From this basis, Fo launches his usual messages about social exploitation and capitalism.

Saint Francis Goes Off to Die

Years of poor diet, exposure to the elements, and caring for the sick took their toll on Francis. By his early forties he was in extremely bad health and his eyes were seriously infected with trachoma. Cardinal Ugolino of Ostia, by then protector of the Franciscans, ordered him to seek treatment, and he was taken to a renowned doctor. In the context of medieval European medicine, his problem was believed to be the result of an excess of cold and damp "humors." This was to be remedied with fire, applying a red-hot iron to cauterize an incision made from his brow to his jaw.[18] Before undergoing this dreadful procedure, Francis pleaded with "Brother Fire" to be gentle with him. During the final weeks of his life, he dictated his last testament, underscoring his principles, and once again exhorting the brothers minor to work for food and shelter, begging only as a last resort. He was carried to the mountains seeking the benefits of the alpine air. While there, a group of knights arrived to escort him back to Assisi. The Assisians were worried he might die elsewhere, and they would be deprived of the precious relic of his body (Cardini 1989:263-68). As his final hour approached, he asked his brothers to lay him naked on the ground, for this was the manner in which he wished to die.

These are the salient points Fo takes up in his final episode. He begins by explaining that Francis is now over forty years old and filled with ailments. Yet, ignoring his brothers' entreaties, he continues to work and keep active. He delivers a speech to his brothers on working in order to earn their alms. "We can't expect that poor folk toil for us, and we pay them simply by praying for their souls!" (90). He strives to continue working, but his eyes and other ailments worsen, and he simply cannot. His brothers must carry him to the doctor, since he can no longer walk. As the doctor prepares to cauterize, Francis appeals to the fire: "Brother Fire, be kind, don't make me scream from the suffering, please be gentle, don't cause me too much pain!" (92). In this last scene, Fo demonstrates his ability to play a wide gamut of registers. The mood is somber and expresses true emotion and pathos for the ailing Francis, which serves as a counterweight to the play's comic and farcical elements. By changing tones he gives *The Holy Jester* emotional and intellectual depth.

After a few days of relief, Francis' eyes worsen, and the brothers carry him on a long trek to a famous doctor in Siena. On the way, Francis requests they take a detour and pass by a hot spring in the area. But upon arriving they see a structure around the spring, in the style of a Roman bath. They learn that the local count has claimed the spring for his personal use, and they must move on. The brothers are enraged. "'Calm yourselves brothers,' says Francis in a weakened voice. 'Do you want to start a war for a splash of hot water?'" (94). By depriving the suffering Francis of a simple desire as well as some relief, Fo makes a statement about private property and the selfishness of the privileged.

The serious tone is sprinkled with humor. As Minorites from other places arrive to be with Francis in his final hours, they all kiss and embrace him: "Easy brothers, you're liable to break me to pieces with your love!" (94). At the hospital, a host of wise doctors apply a number of remedies, including leeches, but to no avail. In the evenings there are lengthy discussions and debates over how to modify and rewrite the rule of the order, and Fo pokes fun at the wise brothers who can spew Latin. Finally, with a feeble voice, Francis calls for silence. "Wait and see. By introducing a clause here and a correction there, our rule will be so sweet and watered down, even Venetian merchants will like it!" (96). This strikes a chord with the audience, who express their appreciation with applause.

On the return trip, they find the structure covering the hot spring was leveled by a combination storm and earthquake. When his brothers suggest this was punishment from God, Francis lectures them on the absurdity of such a notion. He explains that if God took the time to punish all those who abuse their power and/or exploit others (*He mimes God hurling lightning*), there would never by a calm sky (98). However, the hot spring is now accessible, and Francis and his brothers are able to spend some time soaking in the soothing water. As they make their way home, each community wants to host them, hoping the saint's body will become their relic. When they reach Assisi and attempt to go to their tiny chapel, known as the Porziuncola, the knights of Assisi come and bring him to the city. They explain people are out to kidnap him in order that he might die and become a relic in their community. Cardinal Ugolino hosts him in his palace. Francis begs his brothers to sing him a song. They sing his famous *Canticle of Brother Sun* (*Laudes creaturarum*), but they use this as a cover in order to allow some of the brothers to sneak Francis out and bring him to the Porziuncola. They lay Francis down to die, and the play ends as Fo sings the canticle.

Re-Presenting the *Joculator Domini*

In *The Holy Jester*, Fo re-presents history by taking a historical figure in a historical context and modifying him to suit his sense of purpose. In contrast to his usual modus operandi, he is challenged with the fact that one of the defining qualities of Saint Francis was his complete absence of confrontation and of criticism, ". . . evil must be neither avoided or opposed. . . . Only through submission to evil is it possible, according to Francis' conviction, for the power of love and obedience to prove themselves" (Auerbach 2003:167). Presenting Francis in Fo's typical satirical register would have been excessively out of character. Fo deftly uses his indexical frame and other means to avoid this while getting his usual messages across. Using Francis' animal allegories as a basis, he has him deliver criticism of human nature indirectly to the wolf and to the birds, rather than directly to people. He has Pope

Innocent III himself mete out criticism against the papacy and the hypocrisy of the Church's wealth. And by inserting a rendition of the Cain and Abel story, he refers, via his indexical frame, to his earlier versions of the reversed tale, as well as to his "Sacrifice of Isaac." Thus he manages to allude to his usual criticism of the fickle and tyrannical, Old-Testament God.

Taking the concept of Francis as *imitator christi*, Fo informs him with his own concept of Christ, as a member of the folk and counterweight to the paternalistic God and official culture. Francis' message of universal brotherhood is colored with Fo's Gramscian notions of hegemony and resistance to class dominance. Furthermore his folk-Francis is for the most part stripped of the saint's asceticism. The historical Francis was said to have added water or ashes to his food, so as to avoid sensual gratification. One Easter day, upon discovering that his brothers had prepared a lavish table with linen and glassware, he admonished them by acting out a positive exemplum. Borrowing a beggar's hat and staff, he waits for the brothers to begin (as they were accustomed not to wait for him), and then enters the abode, playing the part of a pauper. "At his request he is given a bowl, and alone he sits down on the floor and sets his plate in the ashes. 'Now,' he says, 'I am seated like a Minorite'" (Auerbach 2003:169). Fo's saint, on the other hand, heartily eats and drinks as he celebrates with the folk, including with a band of brigands. Fo's interpretation is underscored by inserting a version of his rendition of the wedding at Cana.

Likewise the saint's ecstatic fervor is transformed into carnivalesque mirth. This is part of the carnival images and themes that inevitably frame the performance. Fo's rendition of the wolf harks back to the pre-Christian, mythological register of "Tale of the Tiger," as human and animal interact and communicate with a common language. The reference to a primordial past is taken further when Francis evokes the fire-theft myth, instructing the wolf to use fire and cook meat, in order to please the deity with a primitive sacrifice. The meeting with the pope takes the Bakhtinian-carnivalesque theme to its extreme, by having Francis suckle on the tits of a pig and splatter the refined guests with feces and mud. All of this is visually framed by Fo's backdrop, with witches, naked women, and a dancing pig. Indeed, Francis was a *giullare*, but Fo chooses to ignore that the Saturnalian elements of his *giulleria* were left behind at his *conversio*.

Even after decades of bad blood between Fo and the Catholic Church, marked by biting satires, stinging invectives, and official condemnations, the Church did not take offence at *The Holy Jester*. Italy's leading Catholic newspaper, *L'Avvenire*, wrote that there was nothing heretical about Dario Fo's portrayal of Saint Francis. In fact, the Vatican's critic, Luca Doninelli, suggests the Church should be "grateful" (1999:10). Perhaps the Church authorities came to the conclusion that their diatribes against Fo simply provided him with more ammunition. And with the added credibility by the Nobel Prize, they decided it was best to make peace. Or perhaps Doninelli, who saw the performance, was taken by the genuine affection that Fo expressed for Francis. The remarkable emotion with which Fo sings *The Canticle of Brother Sun* is truly moving and transcends intellectual interpretation.

Notes

1. The performance on the video is actually a composite of several different performances. My thanks to Gloria Pastorino—who was present at the preparations for the performances—for this information.

2. Frugoni is referring to famous frescoes in Assisi.

3. Of course, there were attempts by certain literate court entertainers to distinguish themselves from their humble counterparts in the fairgrounds and piazzas. Later a similar situation developed within the commedia dell'arte, as the more illustrious companies sought to distinguish themselves from lowly piazza performers.

4. This is not to say that Fo's rendition of the *giullare*'s performance itself is not to some degree accurate. For more on this see Scuderi 1998 and 2000a.

5. Francis and his followers referred to themselves as "brothers minor" or Minorites. "Minor," in the sense of "lesser," refers to their desire for absolute humility and poverty.

6. Motley would later become the standard dress of Arlecchino.

7. As late as the 1950s, ethnomusicologists have recorded European folk songs that included the simulation of animal calls.

8. See Cardini 1989:79-80 and Casagrande and Vecchio 1978:248.

9. Cardini points out that there is evidence of Francis' visit in the writings of the al-Kamil's spiritual advisor (1989:198).

10. Cfr. Francis' thought on guiding wayward brothers in his Letter of 1223 (Habig 1983:109-11).

11. For more on the Father-Jesus dichotomy, see Scuderi 1998:68-89.

12. This explains why the same sentence or consecutive sentences will not run across consecutive pages in the citations.

13. For more on Fo's method of improvising and the dynamics of text and performance, see Scuderi 1998:51-67.

14. For more on sexuality and feminine beauty in Fo's indexical frame, see Scuderi 1998:74-76.

15. Whereas "Cain and Abel" was performed as part of the *Poer nano* radio show, a written version of "Isaac" is found among the stories that comprised the *Poer nano* collection (Pizza 1996:275).

16. "Cain and Abel" is not in the published text (1992e), but is in the video performance (1992c).

17. It could be argued that one reason the Church was inclined to support the Conventual Franciscans and eliminate the Spirituals was that, with their vow of poverty, the Spirituals accentuated the hypocrisy of the clergy's wealth.

18. Noting how much more advanced the medicine of the Islamic world was at that time, Cardini comments parenthetically that "al-Kamil would have had something better to offer his strange Christian friend" (1989:263).

Works Cited

Abrahams, Roger D. 1984. "The Training of the Man of Words in Talking Sweet." In Bauman 1984:117-32.

Alighieri, Dante. 1982. *La Divina commedia*. Ed. Umberto Bosco and Giovanni Reggio. 3 vols. Florence: Le Monnier.

Arden, Heather. 1980. *Fools' Plays: A Study of Satire in the* Sotie. London: Cambridge UP.

Auerbach, Erich. 2003. *Mimesis*. Tr. Willard R. Trask. 2nd ed. Princeton: Princeton UP.

Babcock, Barbara. 1984. "The Story in the Story: Metanarration in Folk Narrative." In Bauman 1984:61-79.

Bakhtin, Mikhail. 1984. *Rabelais and His World*. Tr. Hélène Iswolsky. Bloomington: Indiana UP.

Baroja, Julio Caro. 1979. *El carnival: análisis histórico-cultural*. 2nd ed. Madrid: Tauro.

Bateson, Gregory. 1972. *Steps to an Ecology of Mind*. New York: Ballantine Books.

Bauman, Richard. 1984. *Verbal Art as Performance*. 2nd ed. Prospect Heights, IL: Waveland Press.

Beacham, Richard C. 1991. *The Roman Theatre and It's Audience*. Cambridge: Harvard UP.

Behan, Tom. 2000. *Dario Fo Revolutionary Theatre*. London: Pluto Press.

―――. 2001. "Dario Fo, the Commune, and the Battle for the Palazzina Liberty: Involving Community in the Struggle for a Place to Perform." *New Theatre Quarterly*. 17.66:99-110.

Berger, Harris M. and Giovanna P. Del Negro, eds. 2002. *Toward New Perspectives on* Verbal Art as Performance. Special issue. *Journal of American Folklore.* 115.455.

Bignardelli, Ignazio O. 1962. "Una delle tante beffe del Guerrini?" *L'Universo.* 42.1:177-82.

Binni, Lanfranco. 1975. *Attento te . . . Il teatro politico di Dario Fo.* Verona: Bertani.

Brocchi, Virgilio. 1942. *Le beffe di Olindo.* Milan: Mondadori.

Burke, James. 1995. *The Day the Universe Changed.* Boston: Little, Brown.

Cairns, Christopher. 2000. *Dario Fo e la "pittura scenica": Arte teatro regie 1977-1997.* Naples: Edizioni Scientifiche Italiane.

Cardini, Franco. 1989. *Francesco d'Assisi.* Milan: Mondadori.

Casagrande, Carla and Silvana Vecchio. 1978. "L'interdizione del giullare nel vocabolario clericale del XII e del XIII secolo." In *Il Contributo dei giullari alla drammaturgia italiana delle origini.* Rome: Bulzoni, 207-58.

Chancerel, Léon. 1946. *Le théatre et la jeunesse.* Paris: Bourrellier.

Cowan, Susan. 1975. "The Throw-Away Theatre of Dario Fo. *The Drama Review.* 19.2:102-13.

Da Cuneo, Michele. 1893. "Michele de Cuneo. Lettera (1495)." In *Raccolta di documenti e studi.* Rome: Reale Commissione Colombiana, 95-107.

D'Arcangeli, Luciana. 2009. *I Personaggi femminili nel teatro di Dario Fo e Franca Rame.* Florence: Franco Cesati.

Defoe, Daniel. 1975. *Robinson Crusoe*. New York: Norton.

Doninelli, Luca. 1999. "Francesco giullare presunto." *L'Avvenire*, July.

Eco, Umberto Eco. 1983. *The Name of the Rose*. Tr. William Weaver. New York: Harcourt Brace Jovanovich.

Emery, Ed, ed. 2002. *Research Papers on Dario Fo and Franca Rame*. Proceedings of the International Conference held in Cambridge in 2000. Sydney: Red Notes.

Fantham, R. Elaine. 1989. "Mime: The Missing Link in Roman Literary History." *The Classical World*. 82.3:153-63.

Farrell, Joseph. 2000a. "The Actor Who Writes: Dario Fo and the Nobel Prize." In Farrell and Scuderi 2000:197-211.

———. 2000b. "Fo and Ruzzante: Debts and Obligations." In Farrell and Scuderi 2000:80-100.

———. 2001. *Dario Fo and Franca Rame: Harlequins of the Revolution*. London: Methuen.

———. 2002. "History as Tragedy and Farce: Dario Fo and the Moro Case." In Emery 2002 85-102.

Farrell Joseph, and Antonio Scuderi, eds. 2000. *Dario Fo: Stage, Text and Tradition*. Carbondale: Southern Illinois UP.

Ferguson, Charles A. 1959. "Diglossia." *Word*. 25:325-40.

Fo, Dario. 1966-98. *Le commedie di Dario Fo*. 12 vols. to date. Turin: Einaudi.

———. 1966. *Isabella, tre caravelle e un cacciaballe*. In Fo 1966-98, vol. 2, 2-86.

———. 1974a. *Non si paga! Non si paga!* Milan: La Comune.

———. 1974b. "Culture populaire et travail militant." Interview in *Cahiers du cinema*. 250:11-25.

———. 1975. *L'Operaio conosce 300 parole il padrone 1000 per questo lui è il padrone*. In Fo 1966-98, vol. 3, 81-129.

———. 1976. *Il Fanfani rapito*. Verona: Bertani.

———. 1977a. *Il Teatro di Dario Fo*. Televisione RAI. Videocassettes. Includes *Mistero buffo* and *Ci ragiono e canto*. C.T.F.R.

———. 1977b. *Mistero buffo*. In Fo 1966-98, vol. 5, 5-171.

———. 1978. *Here Come the Jesters*. TV Documentary. Swedish Television.

———. 1980. *Storia della tigre e altre storie*. Eds. Franca Rame and Arturo Corso. Milan: La Comune.

———. 1983. *Dario Fo and Franca Rame: Theatre Workshops at Riverside Studios, London*. London: Red Notes.

———. 1987. *Manuale minimo dell'attore*. Ed Franca Rame. Turin: Einaudi.

———. 1988. *Morte accidentale di un anarchico*. In Fo 1966-98. Vol. 7:5-83.

———. 1990. *Dialogo Provocatorio sul comico, il tragico, la follia e la ragione*. Interviews with Luigi Allegri. Rome: Laterza.

———. 1991a. *Totò. Manuale dell'attor comico*. Ed. Liborio Termine. Turin: Aleph.

Works Cited

———. 1991b. *Dario Fo 1991. Storia della tigre e altre storie.* Videocassette. Milan: C.T.F.R.

———. 1992a. *Fabulazzo.* Eds. Lorenzo Ruggiero and Walter Valeri. Milan: Kaos.

———. 1992b. *Il Papa e la strega.* Ed. Franca Rame. 5th ed. Milan: C.T.F.R.

———. 1992c. *Johan Padan a la descoverta de le Americhe.* Videocassette. Milan: C.T.F.R.

———. 1992d. *Johan Padan a la descoverta de le Americhe.* Original paintings and drawings. Turin: Gruppo Ablele.

———. 1992e. *Johan Padan a la descoverta de le Americhe.* Ed. Franca Rame. Published text. Firenze: Giunti Gruppo Editoriale.

———. 1993. Interviews with Antonio Scuderi, October, Milan.

———. 1997. *Quasi per caso una donna: Elisabetta.* In Fo 1966-98. Vol. 11:195-282.

———. 1998. *Il Diavolo con le zinne.* Ed. Franca Rame. Turin: Einaudi.

———. 1999a. *Lu santo jullàre Françesco.* Ed. Franca Rame. Turin: Einaudi.

———. 1999b. *Lu santo jullàre Françesco.* Videocassette. Turin: Einaudi.

———. 2001. *Johan Padan and the Discovery of America.* Tr. Ron Jenkins. New York: Grove Press.

———. 2002. *Il Paese del mezaràt: I Miei primi sette anni (e qualcuno in più).* Milan: Feltrinelli.

———. 2004a. *L'Anomalo Bicefalo. MicroMega* (supplement). N.2, April-May. Rome: *Gruppo Editoriale L'Espresso*.

———. 2004b. *L'Anomalo Bicefalo*. Videocassette (Planet and Atlantide TV). *L'Unità* (supplement). Rome: Nuova Iniziativa Editoriale.

———. 2008. *L'Apocalissi rimandata ovvero benvenuta catastrofe!* Parma: Guanda.

———. 2009. *Sant'Ambrogio e l'invenzione di Milano*. Ed. Franca Rame and Giselda Palombi. Turin: Einaudi.

Foley, John M. *Immanent Art*. 1991. Bloomington: Indiana UP.

———. 1995. *The Singer of Tales in Performance*. Bloomington: Indiana UP.

———. 2002. *How to Read an Oral Poem*. Chicago: Illinois UP.

Forgacs, David and Geoffrey Nowell-Smith, eds. 1985. *Antonio Gramsci: Selections from Cultural Writings*. Tr. William Boelhower. Cambridge: Harvard UP.

Frugoni, Chiara. 1995. *Vita di un uomo: Francesco d'Assisi*. Turin: Einaudi.

Goffman, Erving. 1986. *Frame Analysis: An Essay on the Organization of Experience*. 2nd ed. Boston: Northeastern UP.

Gramsci, Antonio. 1975. *Quaderni del carcere*. Ed. Valentino Gerratana. 4 vols. Turin: Einaudi.

———. 1985. *Antonio Gramsci: Selections from Cultural Writings*. Eds. David Forgacs and Geoffrey Nowell-Smith. Tr. William Boelhower. Cambridge: Harvard UP.

Habig, Marion A, ed. 1983. *St. Francis of Assisi, Writings and Early Biographies: English Omnibus of the Sources for the Life of St. Francis.* 4th ed. Chicago: Franciscan Herald Press.

Henke, Robert. 2002. *Performance and Literature in the Commedia dell'Arte.* Cambridge: Cambridge UP.

Holm, Bent. 1991. "King, Carnival and Commedia." *Nordic Theatre Studies.* 4:111-36.

———. 2000. "Dario Fo's 'Bourgeois Period': Carnival and Criticism." In Farrell and Scuderi 2000:122-42.

———. 2002. "Dario Fo – A Real *Fabulatore.*" In Emery 2002:121-30.

Horowitz, Jason. 2003. "A Prime Minister Cut Down to Size." *New York Times*, 31 December, B1, B16.

Hymes, Dell. 1971. "Competence and Performance in Linguistic Theory." In *Language Acquisition: Models and Methods.* Renira Huxley and Elizabeth Ingram, eds. London: Academic Press.

———. 1975. "Breakthrough into Performance." In *Folklore: Performance and Communication.* Dan Ben-Amos and Kenneth Goldstein, eds. The Hague: Mouton.

Kleinhenz, Christopher. 1989. "Deceivers Deceived: Devilish Doubletalk in *Inferno* 21-23." *Quaderni d'italianistica.* 10.1-2:133-56.

Lambert, Malcolm D. 1961. *Franciscan Poverty.* London: Allenson.

Le Roy Ladurie, Emmanuel. 1979. *Carnival in Romans.* Tr. Mary Feeney. New York: George Braziller.

Levi-Strauss, Claude. 1975, *The Raw and the Cooked. Introduction to the Science of Mythology*. Tr. John and Doreen Weightman. New York: Harper and Row.

Lord, Albert. 1960. *The Singer of Tales*. Cambridge: Harvard UP.

Marks, Denis. 1984. *The Theatre of Dario Fo*. TV documentary. BBC.

Mitchell, Tony. 1999. *Dario Fo: People's Court Jester*. 3rd ed. London: Methuen.

———. 2000. "'The Moon Is a Light Bulb' and Other Stories: Fo the Songwriter." In Farrell and Scuderi 2000:101-21.

Moyers, Bill. 2004. "Who Needs Michael Moore When You Have the *Real* Show?" Christian Science Monitor, 27 July, p.10.

Nissenbaum, Stephen. 1996. *The Battle for Christmas*. 2nd ed. New York: Vintage Books.

Pizza, Marisa. 1996. *Il Gesto, la parola, l'azione: poetica, drammaturgia e storia dei monologhi di Dario Fo*. Rome: Bulzoni Editore.

Rame, Franca and Dario Fo. 2009. *Una vita all'improvvisa*. Parma: Guanda.

Reynolds Bryan, ed. 2003. *Performing Transversally: Reimagining Shakespeare and the Critical Future*. New York: Palgrave Macmillan.

Reynolds, Bryan and Janna Segal. "Friend or Fo, Shakespeare's End Is the Means." In Reynolds 2003.

Richards, Kenneth and Laura Richards. 1990. *The Commedia dell'Arte: A Documentary History*. Oxford: Shakespeare Head P.

Scuderi, Antonio. 1998. *Dario Fo and Popular Performance.* Ottawa: Legas.

———. 2000a. "Updating Antiquity." In Farrell and Scuderi 2000:39-64.

———. 2000b. "Arlecchino Revisited: Tracing the Demon from the Carnival to Kramer and Mr. Bean." *Theatre History Studies.* 20:143-55.

———. 2003. "Unmasking the Holy Jester Dario Fo." *Theatre Journal.* 55:275-90.

———. 2004. "The Cooked and the Raw: Zoomorphic Symbolism in Dario Fo's *Giullarate.*" *The Modern Language Review.* 99.1:65-76.

———. 2005. "Metatheatre and Character Dynamics in *The Two-Headed Anomaly* by Dario Fo." *New Theatre Quarterly.* 21.1:13-22.

Segal, Erich. 1968. *Roman Laughter: The Comedy of Plautus.* Cambridge: Harvard UP.

———, ed. 2001. *Oxford Readings in Menander, Plautus, and Terrence.* Oxford: Oxford UP.

Silver, Marc. 2009. "Merry Krampus" *National Geographic.* December: np.

Slater, Niall. 2001. "*Amphitruo, Bacchae,* and Metatheatre." In Segal 2001:189-202.

Soriani, Simone. 2007. *Dario Fo dalla commedia al monologo (1959-1969).* Pisa: Titvillus.

———. 2009. *Sulla scena del racconto.* Arezzo: Zona.

Straniero, Michele L. 1978. *Giullari e Fo*. Rome: Lato Side.

Swedish Academy. 1997. "The Nobel Prize for Literature 1997 Dario Fo." Press release.

Toschi, Paolo. 1953. "Gli elementi folklorici nella commedia dell'arte." *Arena*, 1:55-66.

———. 1955. *Le origini del teatro italiano*. Turin: Einaudi.

———. 1976. *Le origini del teatro italiano*. 2nd ed. 2 vols. Turin: Bollati Boringhieri.

Towsen, John H. 1976. *Clowns*. New York. Hawthorn Books.

Turner, Victor. 1967. *The Forest of Symbols: Aspects of Ndembu Ritual*. Ithaca: Cornell UP.

———. 1974. *Dramas, Fields, and Metaphors: Symbolic Action in Human Society*. Ithaca: Cornell UP.

———. 1982. *From Ritual to Theatre: The Human Seriousness of Play*. New York: PAJ.

———. 1995. *The Ritual Process: Structure and Anti-Structure*. 2nd ed. New York: Aldine de Gruyer.

Valentini, Chiara. 1997. *La storia di Dario Fo*. 2nd ed. Milan: Feltrinelli.

Valeri, Walter, ed. 2000. *Franca Rame: A Woman on Stage*. West Lafayette: Bordighera.

Van Gennep, Arnold. 1960. *The Rites of Passage*. Tr. Monika Vizedom and Gabrielle Caffee. Chicago: Chicago UP.

Walsh, Martin. M. 1985. "The Proletarian Carnival of Fo's *Non si paga!*" *Modern Drama*. 28.2:211-22.

Walter, Philippe. 2006. *Christianity: The Origins of a Pagan Religion*. Tr. John E. Graham. Rochester Vermont: Inner Traditions.

Wood, Sharon. 2000. "*Parliamo di donne*: Feminism and Politics in the Theater of Franca Rame." In Farrell and Scuderi 2000:161-80.

Index

Accidental Death of an Anarchist, 16, 27, 30–31, 32, 47–48
Al-Kamil, 108, 130n18
Almost by Chance a Woman: Elizabeth, 33n22, 27, 36, 45, 49–50, 109
Always Blame the Devil, 45
Amati, Aantonino, 30
Andreotti, Giulio, 84
anteprologo, 13
Aristophanes, 18–19
Arlecchino, 72, 76n17, 84, 129n6
Auerbach, Erich, 98
Augustine, Saint, 65
autoriduzione dei prezzi, 82
avanspettacolo, 77

Bacon, Roger, 103
Bakhtin, Mikhail / Bakhtinian, 5, 6, 58, 78, 82, 84, 85, 128–29
Bateson, Gregory, 9, 11
Bauman, Richard, 4, 10–11, 32n4
Beacham, Richard C., 71
Beaumarchais, Pierre, 46
Berlusconi, Silvio, 4, 16–26
Bignardelli, Ignazio O., 42–43
Blair Peach, Clement, 31
Bonaventure, Saint, 97
boni homines, 117
Boniface VIII, 46, 124
Brecht, Bertolt / Brechtian, 3, 14, 95n8
Bristin, 82
Brocchi, Virgilio, 42
buffoni, Venetian, 72–73
Burke, James, 53
Bush, George W., 30

Can't Pay! Won't Pay!, 29, 47–48, 82–83
Canzonissima, 48
Caravia, Alessandro, 73

Cardini, Franco, 97, 105, 106, 108, 110
carnival / carnival culture 3, 5–7, 53–74
carnivalesque, 2, 6, 7, 8, 53, 60–61, 81–83, 84, 87, 98, 100, 101, 108, 128
carnival symbols, defined, 54, 56–58
etymology of, 65, 75n7
inversion of social order, 62, 67
new social order, 57
suspension of social order, 56, 60, 62, 62–63, 69, 73
Carnival King / Lord of Misrule
defined, 54–58
and *giullare*, 68–69, 74, 100
as scapegoat, 56–57
Dario Fo as, 78–79, 80–81, 88
saturnalicius rex, 105, 108
Carpi, Fiorenzo, 33n12, 23
Catholic Church, 6, 8, 43, 47, 63–69, 74, 97, 101–104, 129
Centunculus, 105, 129n6
Chancerel, Léon, 33n17
Chiang Kai-shek, 91, 92, 93
Christmas, 64–65
Ci ragiono e canto, 38
Clair, Saint, 102
clowns / clowning, 16, 17, 22–25, 32, 77
Cockaigne, 58–59
tree of Cockaigne, 58–59, 78
Columbus, Christopher, 41, 42, 45, 48, 79
commedia dell'arte, 6, 7, 14, 24, 63, 70–73, 77
communitas 73–74, 82
Cracokis, 83–84
Craxi, Bettino, 101

Da Celano, Tommaso, 107, 108, 124
Da Cuneo, Michele, 41–42
Da Spalato, Tommaso, 114, 116
Dante, 46, 66
Dario Fo incontra Ruzzante, 46, 109
Dario Fo recita Ruzzante, 46, 109
demons / devils, 60, 65–66, 75n9, 67, 69, 72, 73, 81
The Devil in Drag, 36, 46, 47
Di Pietro, Antonio, 47
diglossia / diglossic, 36, 51n1
Dominicans, 101–2, 104
Doninelli, Luca, 129
Durano, Giustino, 77

Easter, 65, 67
Easter Laughter / *risus paschalis*, 67
Eco, Umberto, 108–9
epic, tales / tradition, 4, 11–12
epic theatre, 3–4, 14, 16, 19, 35, 79, 111
Erudite Comedy, 70
Eulalia, Saint, 83
excited delirium, 31

fabulatori, 3, 44, 77, 88
Falcone, Giovanni, 47
Fanfani, Amintore, 16, 26
Fanfani Kidnapped, 16, 26–27, 82
Farrell, Joseph, 38
Feast of Fools / *festa stultorum*, 67
Ferguson, Charles A., 51n1
Ferrara, Giuliano, 27–28
fire–theft myth / Prometheus myth, 7, 89–90, 90–91
Foley, John Miles, 4, 11–12, 14
folk culture, 2, 4, 35, 37–38, 38–39
fool, 6, 8, 24, 69–70, 81, 100, 105, 106, 109

Fool's Play, 67, 69, 81
fourth wall, 9, 14, 35
frame / framing
  defined, 9–10
  carnival frame, defined, 53
  carnival frame in Fo's theatre, 77–83
  flexible frame, defined, 13
  indexical meaning, defined, 11–12
  indexical / thematic frame, Fo's defined, 12–15
  interpretive frame, 13–14
  performance frame, defined, 10
Francis, Saint 7–8, 97–129
  Canticle of Brother Sun, 127, 129
  as *imitator Christi*, 107–108, 112, 128
  as *joculator domini*, 98–99, 103, 105–7, 110, 127–29
Franciscans / Brothers Minor / Minorites 101, 102–4, 109, 111, 125, 127
  Conventuals, 103
  Spirituals, 103
Franco, Francisco, 48
Free Mario! Mario Is Innocent!, 33n9
Freud, Sigmund, 89
Frugoni, Chiara, 8, 97–98, 110–11

Gargantua, 54, 75n6
Giotto, 97, 129n2
giullare
  defined, 1, 6–8, 67–68
  as a *liminoid* symbol, 6–8, 67–70, 74, 80–81, 100–101
  Fo's re-presentation of, 98–101, 110–11
  Saint Frances as / *joculator domini*, 98–99, 103, 105–7, 110, 127–29
Goffman, Erving, 9–10, 13, 32
grammelot, 22, 33n17, 92, 94

Gramsci, Antonio / Gramscian, 5,
  35–39, 50–51, 87, 100, 128
  Marxist intellectual, 37–38
  organic intellectuals, 36–37, 41
  traditional intellectuals, 36–37
grotesque
  in *Accidental Death of an
    Anarchist*, 27
  in *Almost by Chance a Woman:
    Elizabeth*, 27
  in "The Birth of the Peasant,"
    84
  in "The Butterfly-Mouse,"
    84–85
  in carnival culture, 53, 59–60,
    65–66, 72
  in *Fanfani Kidnapped*, 26–27,
    82
  in "The Holy Jester and the
    Wolf of Gubbio," 85–86
  in *L'Apocalisse rimandata*,
    27–28
  in "Lucio and the Ass," 85
  in "Phallicthropic Harlequin,"
    84
  in "Saint Francis Goes to the
    Pope in Rome," 122–24
  in "The Tale of a Tiger," 87–
    88, 93
  in *The Two–Headed Anamoly*,
    18, 24, 26, 29
Guerrini, Olindo, 41–43
guslari / Serbo–Croatian ballad
  singers, 4, 11, 12

Halloween, 59
hegemony / hegemonic, 5, 35, 39
Hellequin, Harlekin, Arlecchino,
  46, 84
  "Phallicthropic Harlequin," 84
Henke, Robert, 72
history, re–presentation of, 3, 4–5,
  39–51, 80–81
Holm, Bent, 78–79

The Holy Jester Francis, 7–8,
  97–129
  "Francis' Harangue in
    Bologna," 114–16
  "The Expulsion of the Nobility
    and the Shaking of the Forty
    Toppled Towers," 116–18
  "The Holy Jester and the Wolf
    of Gubbio," 85–86, 119–21
  "Saint Francis Goes to the
    Pope in Rome," 121–25
  "Saint Francis Goes Off to
    Die," 125
  "The Wedding at Cana,"
    112, 115, 121–22
homines populi, 117
Hymes, Dell, 4, 10

I Dritti, 77
Il Magnifico, 72, 76n18
immanence, defined, 12
Indo-European carnival rites, 53-
  56, 61
Innocent III, 68, 122–24, 128
inversion / reversal, 44–45, 48
*Isabella, Three Sailing Ships and a
  Con Man*, 7, 45, 48–49, 78–80

Johan Padan Discovers America,
  16, 41, 43, 46, 49, 79–80, 84,
  85, 112, 116
John Paul II, 46–47
Jung, Carl (Jungian), 7, 88–89, 90

key / keying, 9, 10–11, 12–13, 25
Kleinhenz, Christopher, 66

Lady Poverty, 106
L'Apocalisse rimandata, 27–28,
  36, 46
Lario, Veronica, 20–24
Lecoq, Jacque, 77
Lent, 65
Levi–Strauss, Claude, 7, 89–90,
  91

liminal / liminality
  defined, 55–56
  liminal *personae* / threshold people, defined, 68
  liminar, defined, 108
  liminoid, defined, 62
Long March from Jiangxi to Yan'an, 89
Lord, Albert, 4, 11
Lord of Misrule / Carnival King
  defined, 54–58
  and *giullare*, 68–69, 74, 100
  as scapegoat, 56–57
  Dario Fo as, 78–79, 80–81, 88
  saturnalicius rex, 105, 108
Lotta Continua, 16
Lysistrata, 18–19

Machiavelli, Nicolò, 70
Mama's Marijuana is the Best, 87
mammuttones, 81
Manuale minimo dell'attore, 40–41, 92
Mao Tse–Tung / Maoist, 89, 90, 94
Marceau, Marcel, 77
Marx, Karl / Marxism, 5, 35, 36, 37–38, 86, 100, 116
masks
  carnival mask, 58–61, 65–66, 67, 69, 72–73, 74
  maschera, defined, 72
  talamasca, defined, 59
Mather, Increase, 64
memory, 88–89
metacommunication / metanarration
  defined, 11
  metatheatre, defined, 13
Middle Ages and Renaissance
  importance in Fo's theatre, 6–7, 36, 45–51, 73–74, 81
mime, Roman, 71
Mistero buffo, 7, 16, 40, 44, 45, 80–81, 90, 99, 109, 111

"The Birth of the *Giullare*," 40, 99, 112
"The Birth of the Peasant," 84
"Boniface VIII," 40, 43, 46–47, 124
"Cain and Abel," 77, 112, 121
"The Massacre of the Innocents," 111–12
"The Wedding at Cana," 33n21, 86, 112, 115, 121
Moro, Aldo, 50, 51n10
Moyers, Bill, 29–30, 34n26
mythology / mythological
  in "The Tale of a Tiger," 88–89, 89–90, 91, 92
  in "The Holy Jester and the Wolf of Gubbio," 121
Ndembu, 56, 57–58
New York Times, 16–17
Nissenbaum, Stephen, 64,
Nobel Prize for literature, 1, 2, 25, 97, 116, 129
Nuovo Canzoniere Italiano, 38

Obscene Fables, 45
  "The Butterfly–Mouse," 84–85
  "Lucio and the Ass," 85
Odilon, 64
official culture, 2, 44, 50, 51
oral tradition / oral performance 4, 11–12, 14, 35, 38, 71, 87
Ostia, Ugolino of, 125

palliata, 46, 63, 70–71
Pantalone, 72
Parenti, Franco, 77
Parmalat, 19, 33n15
Parry, Milman, 4, 11
parti ridicoli, 72
Pinelli, Giuseppe, 30
Piscator, Erwin, 3
Plautus / Plautine, 13, 46, 63, 70–71
Poer nano, 44, 77, 112, 121

Index

The Pope and the Witch, 29, 43, 46–47
popular culture / traditions, 2, 4, 35, 37–38, 38–39
popular performance, 3, 4, 35
Porziuncola, 127
pranks, 41–43, 60–61
Prodi, Franco, 28
prologue / *discorsetto*, 2, 13, 15, 17–18
Prometheus myth / fire-theft myth, 7, 89–90, 90–91
Pulcinella, 79
Putin, Vladamir, 16, 19–20, 21, 26

Rabelais, 75n6
Rame, Franca, 2, 8n3, 13, 16–26, 38, 48, 77, 78
raptus, 30–31
Red Brigades, 51n10
register
   linguistic term defined, 21
   broader connotation defined, 33n16
reversal / inversion, 44–45, 48
Richards, Gavin, 31
rites / rituals
   rites, agrarian / fertility, 53–56, 58, 60–61, 66, 67, 74
   rites of passage, defined, 55–56
   ritual of status reversal 62–63, 66–67
   ritual symbols, defined, 56–58
   sensory and ideological poles, defined, 56–58
Romans, Humbert of, 101–2
Rossini, Gioacchino, operas, 1

Samhain, 59, 64
Saturnalia / Saturnalian, 5, 7, 61–63, 64, 128
saturnalicius rex, 105, 108
Segal, Erich, 46, 63

Shakespeare, William / Shakespearean 44, 50, 69, 70, 100, 109
Slater, Niall, 13
social order and carnival
   inversion of social order, 62, 67
   new social order, 57
   suspension of social order, 56, 60, 62, 62–63, 69, 73
sot / sotie or *sottie*, 24, 27, 67, 81
Stanislavski, Constantin / Stanislavskian, 21, 35
Storia vera di Piero d'Angera che alla crociata non c'era, 45, 118
Story / Storytelling, 2, 3, 12, 19, 21, 35
Straniero, Michele L., 40, 99–100
sufi, 108

Taiacalze, 72, 73
The Tale of a Tiger and Other Stories, 7, 86, 87–94
   "The First Miracle of the Christ Child," 86–87
   "The Sacrifice of Isaac," 121
   "The Tale of a Tiger," 7, 87–94, 119, 128
teatro minore, 77
theatrical accident, 25, 33n22
Throw the Lady Out, 77–78
togata, 46
Toschi, Paolo, 5–6, 56, 59, 60–61, 70, 78
totem / totemic, 62, 86, 89, 93, 94
Totò (Antonio De Curtis), 14
Trevirius, Nicholas, 70
The Two–Headed Anomaly, 4, 15–26, 28–29, 47–48
Turner, Victor, 6, 55–56, 56–58, 62, 66, 68, 73, 80, 108

Valentini, Chiara, 99
Van Gennep, Arnold, 6, 55

variety theatre, 12, 14, 16, 23, 26, 75n15, 77
vecchi, 71, 72

Walter, Philippe, 59, 64
Wendover, Roger of, 122–23

The Worker Knows 300 words, the Boss Knows 1,000, 38

zanni, 24, 71, 72
zoomorphic, 60, 65–66, 72–73, 74, 83–87, 87–94, 119–21
Zuan Polo, 73